*Writing My Will*

# Writing My Will

POEMS AND PROSE BY JUDITH W STEINBERGH

ISBN No. 0-944941-16-8
Talking Stone Press
Brookline, MA 02445
an imprint of Troubadour, Inc.
a non-profit tax-exempt corporation

For a free catalogue, call:
1-800-557-3100
www.Troubadour.org

Writing My Will
© 2001 Judith W. Steinbergh

Cover Painting: Karen Moss
"Passing Through"
© 1986 Karen Moss

Design by Barbara Emmel Wolinsky, Trillium Design

Other Books and Recordings by Judith Steinbergh
*Poetry:*
Marshmallow Worlds (with Cary Wolinsky) 1972
Lillian Bloom, A Separation (1980)
Motherwriter (1983)
A Living Anytime (1988)
*Texts:*
Reading and Writing Poetry, Grades K-4
Beyond Words: Writing Poems with Children (with Elizabeth McKim)
Reading and Writing Poetry with Teenagers (with Fredric Lown)

*Recordings*: (with Victor Cockburn of Troubadour)
Feel Yourself in Motion
Where I Come From! Songs and Poems from Many Cultures
Get Ready for Boston, Songs, Poems, and Stories
from Boston and its Neighborhoods
Walking in the World, Werewolf Under My Bed,
Are We Almost There, On the Trail

*In Memory of*

MY MOTHER, ROZZIE

MY FATHER, MAYER

and for my children and grandchildren
whose minds, journeys, rebellions, and capacities
I admire and treasure,
here is the true and living will.

# Contents

**HEIRLOOMS**
    What I Want to Give Away     11
    What Holds Us     12
    Egret at Ice Pond     13
    Picnic at the North River     14
    At Kezar Lake     15
    Planting Holland Bulbs in November     16

**MY MOTHER COMES BACK TO LIFE**
    Who Wouldn't Believe     21
    Numbers     23
    Hospital Time     25
    Surgery: A Ceremony     26
    Bathing     28
    Surface Tension     31
    Traveling     32
    Forecast     34
    No Answer     35
    Wildflowers     36
    An Excuse     37
    A Small Thing     38
    Beach Walker     39
    My Mother Comes Back to Life     40

**WHAT MEMORIES WILL RISE**
    What Memories Will Rise     45
    Generations     46
    Late August     47
    Nova     48
    January Thaw     49
    Roller Skating on My Daughter's Birthday     50
    Touching Down     52
    Tattoo     53
    Runaway     55
    Burial     61

## TALKING PHYSICS WITH MY SON

| | |
|---|---|
| Talking Physics with My Son | 65 |
| Ceremony : Bar Mitzvah | 67 |
|   Tomorrow | |
|   Charmed, | |
|   Who Calls Down | |
|   After the Service | |
|   Children of Mitzvot | |
| Volley with My Son | 71 |
| Annunciation | 72 |
| Trespassing in Chatham | 73 |
| Welcome to Our Property - A Song | 74 |
| Bench of Dreams | 76 |
| On the Road | 77 |

## THIS WILD

| | |
|---|---|
| Wild Things | 81 |
| Forsythia | 82 |
| Berries | 83 |
| Mockingbird | 84 |
| Blackbird at Easter | 85 |
| Risen | 86 |
| Moonrise at Chatham Harbor | 87 |
| Questions at Kezar Lake | 89 |
| Exploring Neighborhoods | 90 |
| Trespassing | 91 |
| Not Sailing | 92 |
| The Wind | 93 |
| Closer | 94 |

## MEETING THE BIRTHMOTHER

| | |
|---|---|
| Birthmother, A Fantasy at 11 | 97 |
| Her Name | 98 |
| The Letter with No Address | 100 |
| A Letter Comes | 101 |
| Meeting the Birthmother | 102 |
| First Supper | 103 |
| What Takes its Place | 104 |
| Wedding | 105 |

## LONG DISTANCE

| | |
|---|---|
| Heirloom | 111 |
| Long Distance | 112 |
| Lost and Found: A Story | 113 |
| War Stories | 114 |
| Caretaking | 116 |
| Without Names | 117 |
| Barely Holding | 118 |
| April 15, 1996 | 119 |
| April 16, 1996 | 120 |
| Waning | 121 |
| Endangered | 122 |

## THE ART OF GRANDDAUGHTERS

| | |
|---|---|
| Birthday Poem for Cheyenne Rose | 125 |
| Poem for My Daughter | 126 |
| Gender | 127 |
| Berry Pie, Oh Cheyenne | 128 |
| Thanksgiving Ritual | 130 |
| The Art of Granddaughters | 131 |
| Check-up | 133 |
| Directive | 134 |
| First Time | 135 |
| Departure | 139 |
| Long Distance with Cheyenne | 141 |

## WORKING ON WORDS

| | |
|---|---|
| What Becomes of Poems | 145 |
| Your Old Notes | 146 |
| Work | 147 |
| Are You Mumbling to Yourself? | 148 |
| Waiting for the Word to Come | 149 |
| Defining | 150 |
| A Moment in Every Class | 151 |
| Every Poem is an Emergency | 152 |
| Bringing with Me | 153 |
| Advice at the Mill River | 154 |
| June at Last | 155 |

WORKING ON WORDS
    Sous La Causse      156
      The Naming
      The Maker
      The Guide
      Palimpsest
      Signature

ELEGIES
    Retelling the History      163
    Traub, from My Grandma's Words      165
    Henry's Lupine      166
    There's Millicent in the Small Carved Box      167
    Routine for Leon Collins      168
    Elegy for Etheridge      170
    At the Cemetery      171
    Birthday Wish      172

WRITING MY WILL
    Early Spring Walk at the Reservoir      175
    Form and Content      176
    Mammogram      177
    Acupucture of the Broken Heart      179
    Lighting Tapers in Notre Dame      181
    If I Should be Dying      183
    Writing My Will      184
    Bellbuoy      185
    October Song      186

Notes      188
Acknowledgments      189
About the Author      190

*Heirlooms*

# What I want to give away

are certain words
that have run through my life
like weather or tides
repeating themselves;

*godetia* I borrowed once
from a woman, and *galaxy,*
*caesura,* words whose sounds fly
away from their meanings
like blinding sparks

or meanings that have not yet
grown their words, merely
hovered near me with a kind of heat,
and poems I have loved
like sisters, their lines

clothing me in embroidered
cotton skirts, and tart
taste of blackberries
right off the backyard vines,
the smell of the cottage

at Kezar Lake, just opened
in June, a permanent musk
with spiders still curled
in the window frames,
little balls of lace.

Who will have these jewels?
Overlook the heirlooms:
china, silver, rings
for the real treasures
my darlings, believe me,

what I am giving out—
sting, scent, and the estate
of the soul—is the only
testament of worth.

Being of song, mind, and body,
I make my will,
    – Judith

# What holds us
*In Nantucket*

In spring, it is the Scotch broom's
yellow pouch against green buds, still pale,
or the trailing arbutus, some diminuitive bloom,
or the way, when walking, we flush a quail,
the thrum of its wings, or the strange glassy chink
it makes, the certain print of cloven hooves;
we focus down to barely visible things
rustling scrub. In autumn, something larger moves:

the broad back of crimson breaks the air,
beneath are bright stampeding herds of gold;
bare branches, like gray wings of herons, soar.

Color, ranging, loose from its summer lair,
Color, hot, sleek, feral rolls
and leaps into sky from October moors.

# Egret at Ice Pond

An egret stands against its own image
   in the shallows of Ice Pond,
      like a white brush stroke
         repeating itself, a hieroglyph

meaning grace, stillness,
   willing to wait among cattails
      until we believe it is a puff of
         cattail seed on a long stalk.

In profile, the egret's black beak
   carves away a spear of blue water,
      but should it turn toward us,
         hearing an arm brush cedar,

it will be a long straight lily bud.
   An egret waits; it has no limits
      on waiting, no ambitions,
         until it bends, finally,

deliberate as a plié, plucks
   from its own shadow beak
      a slim minnow, rises, unfolding
         its neck like a new fern as it swallows.

The egret waits, bends,
   snatches, and waits.
      What it needs will arrive
         in silence; it is the egret's way

to sense the flash and act.
   We are learning to be still,
      to take on the patience of wildlife,
         of reeds, to lose something of flesh

and thought. When we bend toward
   our own reflections, may we see
      through the shape of ourselves
         to the shine of what must nourish us.

# Picnic at the North River
*for my brother, Cary.*

*This world we live in is but thickened light.* – Emerson

Your birthday.  Mid-October, picnic spread
on a deep red floral tablecloth,
pine needles slant through the air, cross-
hatching our laps, apples, wine and bread.

We are on a knoll under birch and ash.
That special autumn light that floats and sifts,
leans against the trunks, surrounds our hips,
illuminates a cheek, a wrist, a lash.

We shine in ways unimaginable at birth,
and born in the month of molten light,
you held inside you—light with shape and weight,
till you could carve with light and blow in breath.

Shadows shimmer, leaves glint and drift,
the dogs leap after them, their glowing arcs
remain. Yari throwing sticks splits air with sparks
that you will gather. This is your gift.

Below, the golden marsh flows past like flame,
its grasses sigh and undulate in wind,
the river cuts a steel blue smile and winds
away. We're backlit, still, emerging from your frame.

## At Kezar Lake

Consider even the water of the lake,
so still you can see the webs water spiders make.
Sometimes it seals over like a black cape,
sometimes light is strewn across in silver flakes.

At times, milk seems to rise and spread beneath
the surface like oval opals just bequeathed,
or it is crimson lava pouring from the earth,
or gold streamers, ingots in a blazing hearth.

Slate, pewter, hammered as in a fine vase.
Can this be merely water? Watch its face,
all the peaks and birches use it as a mirror,
yet I see through it to its bones. Clearly,
it's less predictable, wilder than night cries,
remaking itself each time we turn our eyes.

# Planting holland bulbs in november

I take them from their brown bag
each somewhere between an onion
and a young girl poking her firm hips
through her thin wrapping, early tulips

or a small weasel's pointed nose
or the tongue of a lizard flicking
out of the tissue lips, its sprout
anxious to be out in fall, late tulips

and daffodils still saffron secrets
inside a Siamese bulb, its two
pointed skulls off in odd directions.
I dig them in and pat down the cold dirt

of the plots, one by the hedge, one by the walk.
It is the burial of the seed, a kind of
sperm in the earth, a continuity
that nods to my faith in my roots,

my house, my survival of the dark months.
I will forget in February where I buried
the treasure and under the gray snow
there will be caves of heat, an imperceptible

movement of the earth, a wandering of roots
so the soil tightens its grasp.
As the ice saws at my window, I will forget
that the earth rolls magenta on its tongue,

bites down on gold until it's molten,
knows the interior of purple velvet petals,
and before I have found my own body
under the layers of clothes and coats,

the bulbs will be shoving their knife blades,
shoving their crisp green stalks
through a thin split in the dirt,
an electric shock, a flame near the face,

a touch on the genitals, they will come up
straight as a sun's ray, and open and open
and open, a hymn to everything:
rivers, geysers, children, love-making

sun, darkness, ice, trowels, knuckles, work,
everything that is buried and reborn,
closed up and opened,
fist, death, and heart.

# My Mother Comes Back to Life

## Who wouldn't believe

in the Resurrection, the whole
kit and caboodle, boulder rolled
back, the body deep in rigor mortis,
frozen and unfeeling as this soil was
all the long winter?
Who wouldn't believe the sacred
body missing, had risen?
Well yes, anyone could have stolen it,
a man with broad shoulders, three
children with a cart, two large buzzards.
In autumn, I'd be as skeptical as the rest,
but not in April, not when out of the lingering
north side snow, out of the shallow grave,
comes the crocus, small and pale
as if the thin skin, the visible
veins of its petals were all
it could muster, forget real color,
when out of the bulb's dim memory of life
buried in the darkest cave
beneath the clutch of ice-death itself,
rises the blade, the bud, the golden portal
of daffodil so open, its mouth exhales
the cold breath of the earth. Andromeda, then,
braids and cornrows of whitebells,
forsythia flinging streamers of the very sun.

Are we ready for the coming? Everything
I know of life's been hidden for a hundred days,
sealed in, sealed under more like my mother,
that permanence we've had to accept.
After the grief of winter,
after only two, three weeks of light,
out of the bony limbs lacing the brownstones
along the length of Commonwealth,
out of those arthritic skeletal joints,

the long thin magnolias unfurl
into flesh so thick you can press your nails
into ivory and violet leaving brown wounds.
So why not Christ? For that matter, why not
look up into the fragile apple blossoms
for the white froth of my mother's hair?

# Numbers

When my mother was dying
she muttered numbers
as if she were balancing
checkbooks at home

under her breath
chanting numbers
like rosaries, and suddenly
out of that dim journey

telling us to sell,
sell something
we'd never know
the answer to:

a stock, a bond, a house,
a bracelet of pearl,
an old gown
of sequin and tulle,

then numbers again
like watermelons in a field
like seeds in a watermelon
delicious and cool

a comfort when everything
else has slipped away;
words gone like fish,
memories passed already

to the next of kin,
even family inconsequential
as weather.
Only the pain attends

while the inside of the body
rearranges itself
cuts new channels
discards the old,

and numbers, their hard curves,
their certain hollows take shape
in her mouth, the Cabalist code
for the Lord, the secret
combination to her life.

# Hospital Time

The wall calendar is prominent as an icon,
a feeble gesture to say: there *is* "time"
to my mother who sleeps and wakes
unconscious of day and night,
who sips through the i.v.,
its drip drip more regular,
more important than the passage
of days, who murmurs,
"Is it night?" at noon, who is traveling
so fast toward something unknown,
a black hole, an unborn star,
that time slows and stops.
The gravity is such.

# Surgery: a ceremony

In their kindergarten, my children
draw Superman over and over
like an exorcism as if they might
save the world with belief:
Superman combating Luthor, fighting
for truth and justice, righting wrong.

*The surgeon washes up;*
*anesthesiologists, nurses,*
*doctors descend on my mother*
*like a motorcycle gang.*
*Knives glint in the glaring light.*

*My mother isn't there.*
*She is in Florida at the edge*
*of a green sea, reading*
*to my children in the sun.*

*Only her numb flesh hears*
*the mumbling. Now*
*it is all blood. Her belly*
*opens and blooms, a red*
*mushroom nudges*
*the darkness away.*

My children paint the big red S,
paint a huge red earth splitting,
the red paint dribbling down
the page onto the floor.

Everything is red, my shoes,
my eyes, the window glass,
the whole distance between
my mother and me.

*Either the surgeon will find
the tumor and sew her up
or he will not; chances are
it will not end happily.
Darkness will return like a tide
and tumors like barnacles
will flourish.*

Underneath their frenzied cloning,
my children know this; the plane
will crash, the train will crumple
into the chasm, Lois Lane will die
and endless circling the earth
won't change it. Under their taut
blue T-shirts, even the little ones
sense the honest-to-God truth.

# Bathing

It was before we took my mother to the sea, but after we brought her home from the Medical Center. Our day nurse, Roberta, a Vermont native, hearty and affectionate, came days, and Angie, came nights. Sundays, we were on our own. My brother, Andrew came twice from Nebraska. Bess, my sister, covered when she could. But usually I drove up from Boston after work on Fridays and tried to get back to town Sunday nights.

At first I was pulled by the rituals of my weekend life, dinner out with a friend, a play or movie one night. I might rummage through the watercolors and drive up to Gloucester. I was resentful that I had to leave these comforts behind, the peace and companionship that allowed me to absorb the chaos of the work week with humor. I also wanted to be with my mother, to bring some comfort to her during her deteriorating health, maybe even repair some of our past differences. After several of these weekend trips, I began to look forward to leaving the city, to being embraced by the gentle Vermont hills. I would stop at the diner north of Concord on Route 89, then head for Winslow State Park and Sunapee, traveling forward and back at the same time.

Eventually, I began to lose touch. The hospital, its waiting rooms, corridors, coffee shop, its intensive care unit and rooms with cream-colored textured wall paper, the lawn in front with two redwood benches, and the woods behind, these things became my world. Nurses, doctors were my familiar faces. We grew solicitous in an odd way, seeking out things we had in common, hobbies, vacation spots, books, and movies we'd loved.

When I brought my mother home, her room with the shades drawn was too confining for me. Each day, I walked past the old farms and newer clapboard houses, the blue trailer with the horse corral, and crossed Route 5 to the Rogers' meadow, smaller now since Mrs. Rogers sold off some of the acres, but still bordered by the windrow of poplars, and now, in late May, a snowdrift of daisies and buttercups. I stared at their lovely sagging red house and imagined spending the rest of my life here, tending to my mother and my garden, observing the wildlife and painting a little, maybe watercolor cards that would be sold in the college bookstores to campus visitors.

What I mean to say is that it's surprisingly easy to pull yourself away from your essential life, or to reconsider what is of value. And the work that has absorbed you, made you livid or given you extreme pleasure, drifts away, becomes vague and irrelevant.

During the weekdays in Boston, I read all of Kubler-Ross. I could reel off the five stages of dying and I was determined to follow my mother's progress through these stages and help her in any way I could. My mother had passed through denial and was into anger. If I were dying, I'd be pissed too. I wanted to say, "this must be difficult, you must feel angry," but I felt like a fool. She might look at me as if I'd lost my mind. I was busy being positive and imaging the healing process. For her, "anger" lasted a very long time. She may have never progressed to any other stage, but one Friday night I arrived tired. My mother was as bitchy as ever, complaining about Roberta, Roberta who loved her like a sister.

I had thought about nothing else all week. "Ma," I said. "You can be angry for the next few months and keep us away from you. You can refuse our need to comfort you and be alone in this illness or you can let us love you. You aren't getting better. You decide." I straightened her sheets, carried her to the bathroom, changed her nightgown, and went to bed.

Somehow that propelled her into something new or freed her from years of resentment. "Come rub my back," she asked me Saturday morning. "Bring those violets closer to me. Roberta brought them yesterday." And on Sunday, "Call Andrew now and let me hear his voice." "Send a birthday card to Bess's twins, I don't want them to think their grandma forgot them."

We ate some consommé together at lunch. A wood thrush rang through the woods and we were silent together letting it make shining concentric circles in the air. "Sweetie," she said, reaching out feebly and touching my hair, "I like the way you're getting gray, in those lovely streaks."

She ate almost nothing now. A few ice chips, a little broth or pudding. Sometimes when I entered her room, she had almost no mass under the thin blanket. Then I wanted to remember her fighting. Today she asked me if she could take a bath. I called Roberta. She said that in all her years of nursing, no one in this late stage had ever taken anything more than a sponge bath. I could see my mother on the bed, silently muttering the word "bath." I offered once more, very nonchalantly, "My mother would really LIKE to take a bath. How should I do it?"

"I'll be there in ten minutes," Roberta said. "Start the bath water and run it tepid." Roberta strode in. She soaked a blanket in the tub and spread it out on the bottom to protect my mother's bruised skin from the hard enamel. She propped two pillows against one end of the tub. She nodded. I lifted my mother from the high bed. She was so light, I thought she might float in the water like a bar of soap. I sat on the toilet and drew off her robe. Roberta untied her hospital gown. My mother barely had a body. It was scarred where they had tried to remove the cancer several times. She could no longer bother with modesty or pride. She shivered. It was very warm in the bathroom and humid from the running water.

I let Roberta place her in the tub. Even a child could step in, but my mother was too weak to raise her legs. She looked disoriented for a minute. Then, the silk of water all around her evoked some vivid memory or pleasure. She leaned back against the pillows, her hair damp and curled at the ends. She dipped her hands in the clear warm water and raised them up a little, letting the water drip through her fingers. She smiled. She did this again and turned her hands down to pat and splash softly like some thin old bird, and then, almost imperceptibly, she began to sing. I was already on my knees sponging water over her legs, but I had to lean in to hear her. Roberta was changing the sheets. I hummed a little too, although it wasn't clear what melody my mother was singing. She dipped her hands in again and let the water make circles on the surface. "This is the happiest day of my life," my mother murmured, letting her fingers form a wake in the bath.

Her body rose in the water, let go a bit. I leaned back, trying to see her better. She had a beauty, not woman, something else. I thought of a water lily bloom, connected by an invisible stem to a dark place, its white blossom rising up, up, opening to the light.

# Surface Tension

Paddling the outlet, its banks slowly closing in,
you might see through water to the stems
of pickerel weed and lilies, see the river grass bend
in the slow current, the curve of sunken limbs,

the decomposing leaves; their breath escaping
breaks the surface tension, and boulders far
beneath us rise suddenly to dent and scrape;
see how depth is shallow and can scar.

Beyond, it's all opaque, black and glazed,
the boat presses, bends the liquid. Leaping
water striders quilt the surface. Amazed
birch and maple reach, reflect, so deeply,
they pull the sky up from the other side
of earth, that other sky, below the riverbed.

# Traveling

She wants to go to the sea. Outside the window, the bare trees redden on the Vermont Hills. And in the hazy valleys, willows begin to yellow. She is a leaf herself. When I lift her from the high white bed, she is almost weightless. Sometimes I go into the hall to catch my breath, to try to absorb that I am the daughter of this woman who is partially light.

I ask the day nurse what she thinks about making a journey to the coast with my mother.

"It will be very hard on her," Roberta says. I make no response. Roberta is massaging my mother's shoulder, her thin blue arm. "She grew up by the sea, didn't she?" I nod. "Was it near Bath?"

"Yes, did she tell you that? In Georgetown, actually. My grandparents moved there from the city just after the war. We often went back there when we were young. There's a beautiful beach nearby, at the state park."

"If she really wants to go and you're willing to risk it, you ought to give it a try."

Doctor Reed stops by. The i.v., the monitors will be problems. Doctor Lynch returns my call. Pneumonia is a danger. The blockages might grow worse. It depends what we want for her. What *we* want for her?

I sit by the bed of my mother whose skin is already transparent. Her delicate bones pull tight the freckled flesh of her cheeks.

"Is this what you really want to do?" She nods. Barely. "Do you know what might happen?" But no more words come out and inside, I say yes. I do.

She says in a voice so thin, it might be air in aspen trees, "It will be fine. I want to go to the sea, to touch the water." This tires her and she closes her eyes.

I call my sister Bess and my brother Andrew. They can be here tomorrow. We will go on Tuesday. I call friends in Boston. They'll meet us at Plum Island, the barrier sand bar that protects Newburyport. We will have to carry her across the beach.

Andrew was here two weeks before. Now the body of our mother is so much less than it was, to carry her seems like nothing. We can make a sensible plan, but if her life can't complete this journey, how will we respond?

Bess arrives that morning. It is a soft spring day. A day when roses begin in Boston, but here it is still rhododendron, azaleas, tulips. Roberta slips a flannel bathrobe around my mother's shoulders. The slippers hang off of her frail feet. Roberta turns her onto one side and spreads a blanket, then a sheet beside her. From the side, there is no sign that my mother is breathing. Her white hair is matted against one cheek and flattened to the back of her head, which also seems flatter than before. I remember her with wings for hair. The gray-white waves brushed out like gulls.

What on earth are we thinking of? Andrew stands half facing out to the hallway. Bess bends down and gently combs my mother's hair. Roberta kisses her on the forehead. She whispers that she will see her tomorrow. Say hello to the ocean for her. Bring her a shell.

My mother is Roberta's child, and Roberta is preparing to lose her. Soon I will be a motherless child. The song pours into my head like amber molasses, like the wailing healing blues.

I touch Andrew's shoulder. He looks around puzzled as if he'd forgotten our plan. We turn my mother onto the blanket and sheet and wrap them around her. My own infant was delivered to me this way, wrapped in pink lace and blankets. I wondered which end was her head.

Andrew kneels down by the side of her bed. He bends over and his forehead touches where her thigh would be under the white blanket. He stays that way for what seems like a very long time, rocking slightly. Then he straightens up. He puts his arms under the blanket and stands up. She is small and limp like someone who has already died, or is just born. One blue terry slipper falls off. Bess picks it up. My mother's head presses into Andrew's shoulder, her white hair disappears in his white cotton shirt. She smiles faintly. She is leaving home. She is leaving for the sea she loves, grit and salt, pebble clack and tides, sea froth and kelp hold, words that endure.

Bess drives. Andrew stares at a map he doesn't need to use. In the back seat, I hold my mother. I cradle the life in her. I breathe for her. I breathe until the salt comes in and I know we will arrive. Then my mother says, thank you, soundlessly, the way water seeps into and darkens sand.

# Forecast

In the dream
she'd already died
and my service for her
was scheduled for sunrise
on a rock cliff over
Penobscot Bay.
The trumpeter played
Mozart, his notes
clear as petrels
in the salt air
sustaining the dream
until a stranger's face
lifted the flap of our tent
to say
she *had* died.
I was awake
and not surprised.

# No answer

This is the third time this week
I've tried calling you
down under the ground.
This has got to stop.
I know you don't pick up
the phone, in fact, there's no
number listed, but this connection
we've had for years
first umbilical
lately over the wires
is hard to break.
Who else cares
about the kids' first day
of school or my electric bill?
I phone you up in the heavens
but it's no dice,
I'm not into the afterlife
and your burial pursues me
without mercy,
I know you're down there
MA
answer me.

# Wild Flowers

Notice the way the daisies border roads
in Vermont, as if the petals might remain
as snow, or how milkweed in pale pink clouds
outlines the lush potato fields of Maine.
See how the lupine takes the bluest stain
of sea and leaps up painting the sky's edge,
how berry blossoms in the high terrain
survive to decorate the granite ledge,
even the vetch catches the passing eye,
softens the highway with a silvery haze,
and trolley tracks are marked with chicory.
It is left for us to notice and to praise
the hand that leaves its unmistaken trace,
and out of asphalt pushes Queen Anne's Lace.

# An excuse

I slam my thumb in the car door.
In the cold night I cry out
like a wolf that has held back
all this time waiting for the cue.

I fling my voice like a bottle
into the vacant street, against
the hydrant and the concrete steps,
the bicycle crippled on the porch;

everything opens and everything falls
apart, blood vessels split like ships
breaking up at sea spilling their cargo,
bones have a private reckoning.

My mother burst inside like a frozen pipe
and I cry for her finally as I will again.
Upstairs, my children moan and turn,
my hand throbs and stiffens.

# A SMALL THING

I am dozing in my room in late April.
Outside the afternoon sun makes the tulips
yawn so wide you wonder how they will ever
close their mouths tonight.

Inside, nothing is on my mind,
sleep comes in and out like waves
in rock cliffs filling every part
of me then falling away

when the bedroom door taps
or rather swings gently against
the jamb, moved by a breeze
from my window and that small sound,

impossible to describe its softness,
brings me to my mother, not really
my mother, but her bedroom door
which seemed to kiss its sill

all through the hot summer nights
while I lay sweating in my own room
on percale sheets only feet away,
not yet separate enough to close

my door. Now it taps, a gentle mallet
on the stuck gate of my brain
and she is back, voice, hands,
her particular motions, her skin.

Behind my door, my mother sleeps,
merely sleeps, and I could believe
that in the morning, with graying hair
flattened by the pillow, she will wake.

# Beach walker

I am on the beach sinking a little each step looking
first toward the sun which burns down on the front of
my right shoulder pulling the pale skin toward it
then at the tide line where the tiniest shells
have opened their pearly hearts, slate blue,
crimson, peach, and gold. I bend and gather them
in my palm, walking toward the far jetty I never
seem to reach, the beach my mother walked year after
year and I miss my mother; the brown freckled arms
of older women walking toward me look like hers,
the short white hair of the woman I follow makes me
hurry a little to catch up; she is walking here
with me, not diffuse as salt air, not a spirit gliding
like a heron, but a thin brown woman walking with
determination and even steps, a woman whose anger
is subdued a bit by heat and tides, whose freckles
rise to her shoulders like schools of fish: my mother
is walking beside me, we do not need to speak.

# My mother comes back to life

My mother comes back to life
these last two weeks at night
looking for my dad,
puzzled over his new wife.

It is two years and my missing her
sharpens; in my almost sleep
I feel her death
as if for the first time.

I brush my hair and go to the rocks.
At low tide, the seaweed parts
and drapes the ledges.
Underneath everything closes up

for a while: mussels,
periwinkles, feathery barnacles,
and when the tide returns,
they open and eat again.

She could have died
for a time and tired
of the dark, moist silence,
healed and opened.

My back is taking warmth
from the rocks. I try to recreate
last night's black dome
and the vast white drape of light

brightening at its hem until
I had to back away
to avoid being swept in,
then the light pulsing up

the night walls into the crown
of sky like sea swells, jellyfish,
gauze banners in wind,
faster, like heartbeats

until the hummingbird wings
of light beat upward
and it seemed something would open—
a voice huge as horizons would speak.

What we, the living, know is nothing.
We see a bird and name it osprey.
We shape a scallop in our palm.
We try to draw the Northern Lights

a heaven of veils opening and closing.
We, like minnows under Victoria Falls
watch the torrent of light pour upstream.
Or over us, bright salmon

leaping toward the spawning grounds.
By day, we don't even know
what we saw: ions, a field
of magnetic energy, a language

from a distant galaxy, a code
from inside us, thunderous joy
or pain, or all our deceased—parents
and children, dandelions and goldfish,

diffused into light, romping
over the blue black
shell of the universe.

*What Memories Will Rise*

# What memories will rise

Parents are a strange lot, we make
our children's memories like a quilt,
choosing the fabric and the color. We shape
the pattern. As they grow into adults

we hope they'll wear around them as a charm
the heat of ledgy rocks along the coast,
acres of sharp raspberries at the farm,
the bang of a screen door in the summer dusk.

Will they tell their sons and daughters of the taste
of wild blueberries in a pie,
of the night I woke them and we raced
to see Perseid showers in the sky?

Will the scent of lilac bring them back
to their cluttered dressers full of blooms,
Will they hear their skis in frozen tracks
or see the froth of beach plum over dunes?

What memories will rise like slow whales
breaking the opaque surface of their age?
some boy, we never knew of, who once smiled,
the heartbreak of an empty cage,

the way a face swelled from a sting,
a vision of a car just overturned,
kites lost in trees, birds with broken wings,
how maple leaves shrivel before they burn.

Nightmares, pleasure, passion, they'll forget
the way the ocean ferry soothed their hearts.
What they do remember will be hot,
sweet, bitter, sharp, brilliant as fire sparks.

# Generations

In this old snapshot,
I am in the middle of the couch.
On my lap, a tiny baby is
propped up like a Buddha
in yellow bunting.
My eyebrows are raised,
my whole face surprised
as if the mere idea
of me as a mother
were more than my face
could contain without
widening out, opening
up a bit.

It is my daughter
I am holding
as if she were a plant
I might offer the person
snapping the shutter.

On the left sits my mother
actually looking happy
for a change, every silver
hair in place, a pink
apron over her navy shirt
and slacks, her hand
reaching over, touching
the baby's foot. On the right
sits my grandma in a pale
blue suit. Her nylons shine
on her legs and her white hair
curls thinly around her wrinkled face;
her hand grasps my baby's other foot.
Four generations of women,

my dark hair, a kind of sheet
that separates and holds
us together, linked
by hands and those little feet.

# Late August

In the dark, invisible crickets seem to be
sawing themselves in half. We creak and swing
on the front porch, my children reading to me
from separate books, so loudly, there's no hearing
what words they say. The full moon's close
enough to listen, our circle is complete;
this must be the *Saturday Evening Post*.
The proper phrases surface and retreat.

I don't want this fragile night to end.
Soon I will tell you, daughter, that your friend
who coughed and struggled for ten short years, has died.
This very moon that takes away the tide
leaves us here on the summer's shore. Blessed,
we witness the changing season as its guests.

# Nova

School's out, the girls are in the door
jackets, bookbags dropped as if they
were glaciers at a terminal moraine
and in an instant, they are before the mirror

worshipping, besides God, whom they may
or may not believe in...make-up
glistening, velvety, lush, creamy
red and peach. Gloss, enamel, blush,

the silky nubs of brushes and puffs.
Who can blame them? Desperate for
and terrified of boys' lips,
they trace their own curves and peaks

and rub translucent cheeks
with powder of iron and mica chips
until their hot sun rises, and they glow
with such heat, we have to step back a bit.

Blue shadows over the lids like clouds
over the east side of mountains, and below
the eyes are drawn out like the smooth
banks of ponds, and now they'll wait.

It may be minutes, days, months;
meanwhile, they flip their skates
over their shoulders and melt
through the winter streets, separating

the crisp air, leaving a trail of steam.
They are the planets just forming,
turbulent and bright, they orbit
what draws them, what holds them.

Years from now, after they cool,
they will be our beacons of the night.

# January Thaw

Skating tonight, my daughter
wants to take my hand, breaking
briefly from her adolescence.
For months, we've fought
like mothers and daughters do,
the ice forming between us,
thickening, growing opaque.
At night, I bend to kiss her—
she turns her cheek away.

Now the moon's a sliver,
a skate blade thrown down
on the blackest ice.
My daughter, the youngest
of women, glides toward me,
glowing with cold and heat
that meet somewhere as light
just below her skin.

She reaches her hand out,
pulls me along faster
than I can really skate.
I find my balance again.
We are leaning, shifting
our weight together,
laughing, our white breath
better than words,
marking the brittle night.

# Roller skating on my daughter's birthday

round, round and the music
so loud, the sleek maple floor
throbs in a darkness
that eclipses day,
a mirrored ball spins
throwing flakes of light
about my skates, circling
I catch glimpses of the girls
from my daughter's party
in their tight pants
and earrings. Remember
when they came to birthdays
in their starched dresses
stepping the cake into the rug,
how they cried and threw their toys?
Each is holding the waist of the girl
in front, a train of lovely rumps,
shifting weight from side to side;
they could run their lives alone
they think, and all we can do,
the dumbstruck mothers, is hold on
as if they were our fruit
and we, the fragile stems.
I catch up, reach out, their hips
slip through my palms, they pull
away, and I am circling back
my whole body straining toward
something that lurked in shadows
or sped by, leaning against air
in that old tacky rink in Pennsylvania,
the thunder of skates amplified
under the metal roof, where I was
dying to just brush the sleeve,
only the sleeve of someone
I saw once in the corridors
at school, whose forearms had veins
that stood up like rivers at flood.

Struggling from day to day
was like keeping pace with this
counter-clockwise crowd, impossible
to reverse directions.
What is it like to be inside my daughter,
confined for a few hours by
the rules of the rink,
trying the fancy roller dances,
switch and turn, crouch and slide,
glide the carved oval ends
like a gull, like a girl
full of grace and possibility
soaring toward the oncoming brink.

## Touching down

We touch down in Denver, the front range
visible beyond the plains. My daughter draws
some stares, direct from the East Coast, strange
in her black punk skirt, her leather boots. Eyes pause
on her Sex Pistol's T-shirt carefully slit,
her Dad's old vest, her white spiked hair,
her wooden crosses, pale skin, and black lipstick,
six safety pins dangling from one ear.

Do I step behind her on the way to baggage claim?
Do I answer when she turns to me and speaks
or do I leave a gap, accentuating our extremes,
let stony image play for keeps?

I choose to travel with her and disarm-
ingly she lets herself slow down and take my arm.

# Tattoo

At 14, rumors of
TATTOO
worse in my view
than the punk hair-do,
the black decor
of her room, the torn
outfits, the metal gear
that might disappear
unlike a permanent
ornament of torment
TATTOO
indented black holes
burned through
her still new flesh,
who will do
this sketch
this pas-de-deux
with pin and skin
pricking the dye into
delicate tissue
indelible dye
high on her back
drawing of blood
scarring of body, who?
TATTOO
at some friend's she knew
in Revere–a rendezvous.
Sterile, ha! Peril, she has
no interest in my view.
Something she outgrew.
TATTOO
Imagine, I say,
at 62, skin shriveled,
some image you
thought was cute
peeping over your straps, askew,

youth's residue.
Self-inflicted route
to infection, think
about AIDS
be afraid this time
be afraid, eschew
TATTOO

She twists her lips—
*screw you.*
She turns, tugs down
her shirt from her shoulder,
the blue black head
of a cartoon cat,
two inches of seared flesh,
makes its debut
tongue drooling to the left
big eyes staring
as much a part of her
as an ankle or breast
what survivors dream
of rubbing from the forearm
TATTOO
a cry of alarm
TATTOO
this girl's impervious to harm
and she has follow-through
TATTOO

# Runaway

*The Search*

The daughter is not yet found,
not exactly lost; *she* knows
where she is: quivering, cold,
dreaming of hot coffee,
half sugar, half cream, or
safe in a room her mother
cannot locate, or lurking
in drugstore aisles,
hitching on a highway
toward New York, huddled
in the backs of stolen cars.

The daughter took her make-up,
black jerseys, black skirts,
a nameless boy, her ragged
bear, hair spray for her
spiked-up hair, the slamming
of the doors.

The mother locked the door
and slept.  The mother woke
and searched the cellar
and the sheds, she searched
the hang-outs and the malls,
she called the numbers
on her daughter's walls,
she wept, she called the cops,
she called the rescue leagues,
questioned street musicians,
posted posters, waited by
the entrances to clubs and subways,
to shelters, and at home,
she waited by the phone.  Her life
was a flatland of waiting.

How will they welcome her?
How will they grieve for her?
How will they punish her?
The runaway daughter wearing
an adjective like a leather coat,
is recognizable by the bonds
she broke. She fled the family
with chains of empty lockets,
a fugitive from comfort,
traveling the charmless cities
of the North, leaving the mother
in a paneled landscape, a territory
where weather numbs and the route
is still unmapped.

*Wednesday, August 26*

I tiptoe to the basement, almost certain they have sneaked back in through a window during the night and are sleeping on the couch down there. No kids. I call the police at 9 a.m. An officer arrives. He takes down the information. When I describe her appearance, short very blond hair, black leather jacket, black skirt and black boots, the officer says, is this a fad or something? Does he have kids? I call her dad. I call a few of her friends and make a feeble effort to find out where they might have gone. My lack of energy is uncharacteristic and I'm not sure if this indifference is disguised anger or a parent trying to pull back. My son actually goes back to bed, the first time I specifically observe that the situation is affecting him. My concern for my son is growing. At noon I drag him off. We buy him a new bike and run errands for the house.

Wednesday night, I tell a few friends. You wait on these matters because you think she's really going to show up shortly. It's going to rain in a few hours and she'll show up then. Why make it a federal issue? When you are getting separated, you don't tell your family for a while because you might work it out, it may resolve itself. That way you can avoid having to hear that it was your fault. But she doesn't call.

*Thursday, August 27*

My daughter has been gone two whole nights. It is drizzling. What is she eating? Her father calls. We have a strategy meeting by phone. I say I will go to the Police Station and file the CHINS: Child in Need of Service. He will go to Harvard Square and talk to kids. But it is raining. Will the punks even be out? I call Detective Lamb and set up an appointment. It seems that today is the day I have decided to participate in this. Also it becomes clear, you can call the police and in this town they are attentive and supportive, but figuring it out, looking for clues, is really up to us. Liza calls from Maine. She remembers she has taken a picture of my daughter and her boyfriend on my front steps. The film is ready at the photo store. I jump in the car. I get the pouch of film. I rip it open. There it is! A print of the two kids, vulnerable, not the pose you'd want plastered all over the country. But it's what we've got. It's like *Blow-Up*. I race to the station. My detective goes over the latest material. She looks at the photos. She will make a poster and send it to other communities where we think they might hide. Now Detective Lamb takes me to the Court House. We wait. Finally, the Chief Probation Officer comes to get me. He fills out the forms. I am like a robot, saying her name over and over as if she were just an address instead of a child, a daughter. They type out the CHINS warrant in another office and I must sign it. Another woman comes along to take my oath. I must swear that my daughter has run away from home. Are they kidding? Would I be there? Do I have better ways of spending my time? Maybe they make you swear so that the state is not expending resources in cases where the kids have slipped away for a bit or the parents abdicate altogether. I read the warrant. "...that she has consistently run away from home and disobeyed her parents...we pray the court....." Uhuh. The wall wavers. This could be it. I can't look the clerk in the eye. I raise my hand and say I swear it. I go back into the corridor and wait. The judge has to review the case and decide if the CHINS application will be accepted.

Meanwhile a woman speaks intently with her social worker or lawyer, a child circles her skirt until she is called into the courtroom. Shortly she comes out, lifts up the child and cries. This does it. I cry too. I don't even know what happened. She got custody, she got bigger payments, she adopted a child, she is smiling. The next family goes in. It's drama every four minutes out here in the waiting room. Each of us waits on a bench with her own story uncertain of the outcome. The monitor calls me in. I look around. The courtroom is half full. Everyone is staring at me, a school teacher from this town. Can they tell by looking at me that my child has run away? An oath-taker makes me raise my hand and swear once again that my daughter has run away. The toughness is getting peeled away like onion skin. The judge looks at me kindly. Has she run away before? Yes, once for a night. How old is she. Still only fourteen. It seems as if she's been fourteen forever. Do you know her whereabouts? No. Are you sure? I open my eyes widely. Yes. He looks concerned. He OKs the CHINS. I am done. I go out into the street, shaking, and cover my face with my hands.

*Friday, August 28*

I am beside my son,
peddling the back roads
past the Georgian houses,
past the clapboard farms,
past the sumac turning,
past the summer swarming
into fall, peddling the whole
path around Jamaica Pond,
the water glitter, the gull clatter,
the boats with rowers
still as August, past runners,
*los muchachos* clambering
up the fountain for a drink,
past the boat house and concession,
around the kids at the edge leaning
their lines toward trout,
a girl pressed against
her lover's chest.  Overtaking
the gentle orbits of the elders,
we swerve under dusty willows.
Go ahead!  I'll follow!

We are in our own minds,
our secrets are spokes
that press our lives into
perfect circles, moving
us forward as if everything
functioned as it should.


*"Fortunately the universe is not that complicated."* Steven Weinberg

Strings, bubbles, background static,
galaxies flying away from each other at Hubbell's constant,
quarks strange and charmed, neutrinos
piercing granite as if it were clouds,
and here on earth, two thousand kinds of dragonflies alone,
and true bugs, impossible to enumerate.
A daughter is wandering the steamy city,
eating croissants in the hazy nighttime
among jugglers and clowns, picking her way
through the shifting borders of love.
Sirens and flashing lights trail her.
In the darkness of the country, her mother finds,
through light-gathering lenses, galaxies whirling out
of the dipper's bowl twelve million light years away.
Yet the daughter, where is she?
Staring out into the billion stars, the mother
peers fiercely seeking comfort from equations,
the predictable cycles of suns pulsing and dimming,
positive and negative charges summing to zero,
desperate for a cool explicable design.


*Sunday, August 30*

There are no messages on the machine. It must have malfunctioned. It isn't possible that no one called. My friends arrive with pasta and spicy chicken, a sort of picnic by the phone, and just as we are about to dig in, the phone starts. Heather calls to say a friend thinks she has seen my daughter's boyfriend at a concert last night. My brother checks in to say he has dead-ended on leads and has gone home. My daughter's dad calls to say he has a new lead in Brockton and my nephew calls from another phone to say someone had served a girl who resembles the photo a croissant for breakfast and she had told the waitress she was a vegetarian. Yes. She must be there! My daughter is in hiding, but still out eating her croissants. The Search and Rescue kids are out in force and Elaine, their liaison, is lying on her bed somewhere, ice pack to her head, manning the Search and Rescue phone.

We eat the chicken. They have another lead. We eat the pasta, they have the name of the place she works. We drink some wine. They finally reach the owner who might know where my daughter is living. The drama intensifies. They call again. They have an address, are heading out to swoop in. We eat dessert. An hour later, my nephew, Stevie, calls. We have her Aunt Judy. He sounds completely exhausted. I start doing dishes, finishing laundry as if I'll never have the chance to do housework again. Liza and I make up my daughter's room so it will look welcoming. I walk out to the porch. I march anxiously around the house. I call my closest relatives to say she's been found. I review all the phrases I've arranged in my mind to see what I will say when she arrives home. I try to imagine what will happen next.

It takes longer than I think to bring her home. When she bends out of the back seat, Stevie is holding her up and she is laughing. I didn't expect that. I give her a kiss and murmur that I am so happy to see her. She clings to her cousin who carries her up to bed and puts her in. Her dad comes into the kitchen to review the days events and the shock of having the police process take over what needed a family solution. The actual encounter with authority might deter a child from running again.

Liza and I sit on the edge of my daughter's bed. She chatters away about her adventures as if she's just returned from overnight camp. She loved the people in the house where she was sheltered, they took such good care of her. Belinda had kissed her every night, she almost had a job, and she cooked and cleaned and helped take care of Cindy's baby. Like being independent, playing house…she didn't really miss me and anyway didn't Renée call to say she was OK, wasn't that enough? …and then she fell asleep.

# BURIAL

It is Sunday, day of rest. My daughter is out, her pet rat
is scratching in his cage, rotund and senile, sedentary
and smelly, the darling of my daughter's life. I am paying
my bills: electric, water, news, throwing a little money at
my charge cards, trying to figure how the gas company got
control of my life; writing, tearing, licking, sealing,
when I reach the phone bill, the total, second only to
the national debt, the decimal point lost among all those
digits, numbers that repeat like rain, numbers my daughter
has gleaned from movie magazines, rock star rags, and friends
of friends, calls to Hollywood, Memphis, Staten Island,
San Diego, Juarez. My breathing is heavy,
my blood rises like the Charles in spring.
The door opens and bangs. My daughter is there
in her leather and make-up, my daughter, wearing black,
steps into trouble. I show her the bill. She doesn't know,
she says, her friends must have used our phone, she says,
she'll never touch it again. I am shaking, my hands have a
strange attraction to her neck, I am clutching them behind
me when—the rat dies—and indeed, the bloated rodent
is flat on its side, little claws curled permanently around
the air. I am a train that must brake for a cow. I am a plane
landing at an airport that is closed. My anger skids on the
asphalt. Funeral plans must be made. My daughter is wailing
like an ambulance, stroking her pet's cold snout. We
prepare a silken shroud, a cardboard coffin, we say our last
good-byes and seal it in with packing tape so cats won't
scratch it out. I dig up old snow under the cherry,
a prime resting spot, I dig as deep as strife. We lay
the box among dark clods of dirt, sprinkle topsoil on, say
our prayers and psalms, poke in dried flowers and a cross
my daughter's borrowed from another site. I stare at her across
the yard's scar. If she hadn't loved that rat so hard,
I'd swear she planned its death. The phone bill waits,
still fresh, but I have buried the sharp claws of my anger,
its ugly tail. What is lost is something small and warm
I nurtured once, something I thought was my own.
My daughter goes inside to get the phone.

# Talking Physics with My Son

# Talking physics with my son

David reads the sports page holding it up like a man
and to the side of his French toast plate with a gravity
that makes me smile. His compact body defines his space.
Watching football on TV, in the pale violet light,
he shouts, his fist punching the air. After school, my son
lies in the dirt shooting marbles or runs against his record time,

yet pronouncing his French, he sits in my lap. What a time!
Ten. A treasure stumbled over in the midst of a woman's
life. A flame inside beveled glass pushing at the night, a son
orbiting me and this table where I sit as if our mutual gravity
would keep him circling forever, pulsing with some inner light.
You know the way young boys can't stop moving when they talk, they space

out, jiggle like molecules, hang from door ways, legs dangling in space,
chattering about energy and mass, $e=mc^2$, how time
is relative, can't be counted on to proceed in a line, and light,
the only constant in our lives, more constant than women or men,
can actually be bent from its path by gravity
so *where* we see the stars is distorted by the force of the sun

in fact, how he and I observe a star, or galaxy, or sun
may differ depending on our speed or where we are in space.
As I said, it's all relative! Moreover, gravity
not only pulls our blood and tugs at tides, but slows down time.
Flowers grow—iron rusts more slowly and if David manned
a spaceship traveling the universe near the speed of light,

he might reach Andromeda, discover new life, alight
on a green lush planet, looking back at our own faint sun
and a white-haired mother while he remains a young man.
How this child is seen, how he proceeds through life, his space-
time continuum, the path he takes…only time
will tell. I might bend him towards me a bit with my gravity.

The shortest path between birth and the carved date on the grave
is not always what it seems. Divergence, enlightenment
intervene, pushing out the edges of the mind. One at a time,

revelations unfold in this small tired boy. It's late, the sun
has set already, all this heady conversation, this space-
talk, this avid fascination with a brilliant man

is engraved on us like an equation. Pull the quilt up, son.
I'll turn out the light. You're drowsy, but your mind still speeds through space.
It's time for sleep. Thank you God or Einstein for this child. Amen.

# Ceremony

*Tomorrow*

is my son's Bar Mitzvah.
The week, sealed in rain, splits
and sun floods in. A rose
I predicted in March opens,
trolleys rumble past, cars
blare raps and carriages
rattle over sidewalk cracks.
My family is threading through
the nation, through
this city, finding its way
to the center, the knot.
I am drawing a garment around me.
At some intersection, in some lobby,
I could meet them, aunts from
the heartland, cousins from the margins
of the continent, but I make myself
sit on the brick step alone, still
and powerful as a magnet. I have done
all there is to do, dug even a trench
around the garden, and soon
this thin mortar of peace will dissipate,
the family will form itself again,
the ancient ritual begin.


*Charmed,*

the day blew in like a bright bird,
I lay under cool sheets while local wild life
celebrated with early prayers and psalms.
I bent to wake my son, invisible under the red
striped quilt, the Bar Mitzvah boy, a bodiless puff
of *haftorah*. I threw open windows and doors.
June was there, the first guest, bringing her roses.
Muttering lines, we dressed, and when we were perfect
and rehearsed, we stepped into relatives and flowers,

stood with the rabbi and the choir,
drew back the velvet curtain of the ark
and blessed Torah and held high Torah,
its weight upon us, its words, breath, spark,
unscrolled for the boy in the pressed suit,
himself unfolding into the man
who would chant the sacred text.


*Who calls down*

the spirits of the dead?
The cantor chanting mourner's *kaddish*
winds them in like distant specks
of kites on taut familiar lines.
A grandson in a trim gray suit,
a daughter in a wide-brimmed hat,
expect their arrival. So they come,
like ordinary guests,
checking into rooms,
their names on the computer list.
Such is the power of the day,
the tug on the dead and the living,
the infants suck in silence,
the toddlers stay awake
waiting to close the ark
upon the scrolls,
and the unborn turn in the womb
anxious for their portion
to be unrolled.


*After the service,*

my mother flew around the balcony,
the dome, growing larger, filling
the room; a wind, pale and wonderful
bent the pews, she swirled away dust,

drapes, crumbs of *challah*, hats
of surviving relatives, thoughts
of strangers who unconsciously
reached into air; my mother

swooped out of the heavy sanctuary
doors, trailing the final adoration,
drowning the blessing over wine,
leaving a kind of vacuum behind,

raced up Beacon Street, wove
through the trellis, slipped
between the clapboards of the house
so carefully prepared for her,

straightening the immaculate rooms
for the imminent arrival of the guests.


*Children of Mitzvot*

They bring us back to each other
like shepherd moons, They make us
see our deepening creases,
They stand on the bima
singing alaynu, praise
with our faces or our voices,
our gestures or a phrase
that echoes someone we have lost.

Called and honored with aliahs,
their grandfathers and aunts,
sisters and parents, chant
and touch their shoulders
lightly. In this way,
a tallis of wisdom is woven
around the body of each child
who celebrates before the ark.

They travel the passage of Torah,
the Talmud's complex maze that says,
"Begin anywhere." And they do,
carrying with them our odd smiles
or freckles. In their pockets,
fragments of family myths
glitter like mica, soften like talc.

We are no burden to them;
our feuds and favorites slide away.
To them, we are the warp and weft
and fringe, we are a fine wool comfort.
They step into our future,
shining, intelligent and clothed.

# Volley with My Son

Once again we are at it
whacking the frail basket
of the birdy through the air,
the fourth June we have stretched
the sagging net across our yard
to be where roses are profuse,
where honeysuckle leaks out
into the thickening dusk.
We are getting better, each year
the birdy sneaks through the net
fewer times, thwacks the wooden
frame of the racket less, swooshes
then hesitates in air, the way
it should, like a gull considering
a glint under the sea. We reach,
run, smack, talk of Plato, Sophocles,
where they converged and disagreed,
how Alexander, valiant soldier,
loved a man, our eyes steadily
on the birdy, we do not let it drop,
how tough and tender he was, we
know we will jinx the volley if
we even mention it's been going on,
the trick here is to attend with
the sight to one thing and with
the mind to the other and both,
then will fly, will fly.

# ANNUNCIATION

I hear through my son that his father's new wife
has bought a book of names, and yes, we have speculated
all along there would be a baby—when she was done
with school, when business started looking up—
but nonetheless, I am caught, my breath sharp
as wind when weather changes, and I am thinking
how should I feel, while I am feeling what should I think,
and my son says, it's too late anyway, *he'll* be off in college
by the time *it* speaks and *it* better be a boy.

Later I learn, it is not the first and I find I want
this baby to stick, not like all the seeds in me that slipped
away, and I lean toward this woman in my dreams
as if she were my daughter or my niece, and her child
would carry something forth of me.

I find the wicker cradle, pushed to a shadowy corner
of the basement, filled with old pillows and listless bears,
the cradle where our children slept when we adopted them,
eighteen, then sixteen years ago. I wash and line the wicker,
buy a flannel sheet, a hand-stitched quilt. Your child, now,
will babble and dream, finger the sunlit air, lift its eyes,
scream, where its sister, then brother once lay, fidgeting,
playing with rattles and colorful squares, all of us
forming our mouths into O s, astounded at what
we have brought, one way or another, into
the fresh white wicker weave of family.

# Trespassing in Chatham

All day my son and I are biking narrow roads that rim peninsulas and shore,
    catching glimpses of the sea, its broad glitter, the indefinite bars,
but we are disconnected from the continuity, the tides, by private property,
    signs, gates, warnings, the massive shells of homes too big for families.

We find a Wildlife Refuge on our map, but no access. The U.S. Geodetic
    shows there used to be a path. We nose down driveways and side yards,
brush verandahs and porticos for Porsches, discover a track, overgrown, steep,
    eroded, and a rusted sign, *Heron Trail*, then a tasteful *Private*.
Down these grassy ruts, we walk our bikes, tilting back, stalking past a terraced
    lawn, past gardeners spreading mulch through swamp oak and maple.

Poison ivy closes in, clues us. Beyond, a large blue sign erupts from a dune:
    WELCOME, and just below, *Closed from Dusk to Dawn*.
"Your legacy, my son. A coastline you must enter like a burglar." We lean
    our bikes on cypress, sink into swells of dunes, wade in the back coves
of Stage Harbor, witness egret and hawk. Return

when you need to, my son. Trespass fiercely with determination,
    trespass gently with consideration for mollusk and tern, disdain
the words that keep you from refuge, from a necessary breath of peace.

# Welcome to our property — a song

Welcome to our property,
welcome to our piece of waterfront.
Avail yourselves of shade and sand,
have a picnic anytime you want.

Please take a swim, please dry your skin,
enjoy our hard-won privacy,
and when you're feeling like our kin,
come up to our house for some tea.

> We're just the fortunate few,
> We have the very best view,
> A piece of wilderness, too,
> We want to share it all with you.

Welcome to our property,
We'd never post one of those hateful signs,
Do Not Trespass is oh so crass,
Your pleasure's foremost in our minds.

Welcome to our tidal marsh,
get away from tourists on your bike,
you'll hear the gulls and grebes, but nothing harsh,
you'll feel what privilege is like.
*chorus*

Don't miss the sunset on the beach,
the fireball spreads its coral light,
Don't miss the dawns, don't miss our lawns,
Don't miss the galaxies at night.

And bring your friends and bring your Coors,
and bring your family and pets,
As Woodie says, "this land is yours!"
We plan to share our benefits.
    *chorus*

You think this set-up is unfair,
wrong name, wrong color, you're too late,
You wonder if you'll get your share,
It's time for us to compensate.

We have the silver tea set out,
the gardener's trimmed the whole estate,
when you arrive, just give a shout,
we have our finger on the gate.
    *chorus*

# Bench of dreams

For his sixteenth birthday, my son asked for a set of weights and a weight bench. He is a young man with few material demands, a thoughtful person, an athlete devoted to track, so his father, his father's wife, and I chipped in for the big one. His father chose it, a massive black rig with a black imitation leather bench which allows you to lift with your arms and legs at the same time, should you ever be so inclined, a matte black lifting bar and fabulous gold weights. The weights were packaged efficiently in a small box separate from the disassembled bench. It was almost impossible to lift the weights, boxed together as they were, out of the car. My son's father seemed to be eager to set it up at his apartment, just try it out, see how it felt. A weight bench he had always dreamed of, rather than the hand-me down minimal red thing from George. His wife, fully aware of how the weight bench might become a permanent fixture, convinced him to leave the gift in its boxes for our son to unwrap himself. My son was delighted with the gift, eager to have it installed in his bedroom. Bedroom! I had pictured the basement, a spacious room of concrete where boys could congregate to sweat and groan, a floor that could handle the accidental drops of 200 pounds of weight. My son prevailed, would he really lift weights in the dead of winter if they were ensconced in the cold dark basement. Why not have them nearby, as a break from...his studies.

The following Sunday his father came to assemble the apparatus, a nightmare of screws, nuts, unfamiliar steel tubes, with directions written in five languages, none of them comprehensible. I left the house to walk around the reservoir. When I returned, everyone was swearing and taking apart pieces they'd already put together. I left again for groceries. By evening, they'd managed to produce a weight bench of sorts, a little shakier than a mother would like, consuming the generous space between the bed and the closet door which might have opened for the last time. My son and his father were vying for turns, my son's lanky arms, struggling to outlift his father's muscular ones, to claim the bench, his birthday present, as his own.

When his father left, my son closed his door to be alone with his weights and to begin bonding with his weight bench. He was just coming into a man's body, still lean and all one piece, as if the muscles hadn't received their names yet. I pictured him sitting on his weight bench, saying good-bye to his boy's body, one that had so recently been compact enough to curl up on my lap. I'm sure he was thinking of deltoids, laterals, pectorals, shaping himself into a terrain where muscles were defined, separating themselves into ridges, valleys, a new landscape, barely recognizable to a boy's mother.

# On the road

Dave calls.
His voice comes clear or crackling
out of the chaos of hostels or the hollow canyons,
out of the starry darkness of campgrounds,
dew gathering on the mouthpiece of the pay phone,
mosquitoes whining under the dash of the phone booth light.
His voice is his. Hey, ma, he says—as if he'd just bumped open
the front door after school or a long lean run,
only he's on the road, 2 months, 4000 miles away from
the open refrigerator where he bent daily searching for Ginger Ale.
He feeds me stories, images, anecdotes he knows I want to hear,
bison ambling by his tent, the scoop of Crater Lake,
Aunt Betty's all-you-can-eat-buffets; the car's still running,
he's reading Kerouac's *On the Road,* and the rest he shuts
in the glove compartment of his mind.  My son,

the seam opens, it widens, blue sky shines through,
we know we're connected, we both have stitch holes
at our common edges, but the thread's pulled free. Now
there's a ribbon of road, a freeway, Route 66, the Mississippi,
Monongehela, the Snake or Susquehanna, something to cross
or follow, a trail to a peak, a dripping passage to a limestone cavern,
stairwell to a spire, a kiva ladder into a sooty cave, there's smoke, clouds,
contrails, and you are out there moving across the land, across basin and range,
winding between red rock and sage brush, climbing down into the history of
rivers, ascending the elbows of granite jabbing the sky, an eagle surveying
the shape and shadow of our land. Looking inward at the vast expanse
you must travel, you press away from me, even
as you turn toward home.

*This Wild*

# Wild things

What is it that makes us love wild things?
That after long patience and a kind of thirst,
after speculating on the slap of water, whir of wings,
out of the grainy dusk, some wild creature bursts
from the forest. Before we focus on its shape,
almost before it can be named,
it twists back, leaps, makes its escape.
Whatever it was, we know it can't be tamed.

Do we want the whole deer quivering under our gaze,
the fox frozen as a statue in its track?
No. Only the glaze of eyes, the lightning bolt of legs,
the otter's wake. We want the power to attract
wildness. To be skimmed, sensed, not faced.

We want to love wildness, to feel that we've been graced.

# Forsythia

I am never prepared enough.
I think I remember yellow.
I remember sun, butter, lemons, gold,
but today, the 12th of April,

I believe I have never seen this before.
The emergent red halo around the maples,
the chartreuse gowns of willow,
the creamy stars of magnolia withdraw

behind the brash forsythia, exuberant,
leggy, leaping out of the earth
as if the sun had been buried there all winter
and spewed out now from its flat pewter disk

into yellow, yellow, the first
and only event of this color,
yelling about spring, yellowing lawns
and clapboards, slopes and hollows.

Even at night, they smear
the blackness with their graffiti,
they part darkness, they make
a country of midnight sun.

Forsythia is in heat, is heat.
Watch out!  Its tentacles vibrate
the late April air, and if they brush you,
they will shock you awake.

# BERRIES

For this pie, not just any berry will do,
not the fat pulpy, blueberry, inflated and dark,
No, only the tiny wild berry, silvery blue,
brushed with powdery yeast, dew and plucked
after an arduous, breathtaking, terrifying climb
to the very peak of Baldface, where blueberries grow
in such abundance, you step into their sweet wine,
lie in them, tracing the papery hawks, the lakes below.

When you have stripped down, sweating at the mountain top,
when your elbows and knees have taken on their crimson stain,
your thumbs begin to work, roll these tough
berries that rise from ice and lichen, that hold the rock,
that ripen from fierce sun, stinging rain.
These plain, these warm tart berries are wild enough.

# Mockingbird

In my youth, I wanted someone stable as a groom.

Now in these mid-years, let him be extreme, absurd,
bring honey, incense, wear silk capes and plumes,
let him seduce me. Take the mockingbird:
To court, he sings each song that he can steal,
flapping upward, upward in the tree,
wildly singing to the very top, then keels
over, falling backward in a kind of ecstasy.

Now that's style! I've been in love,
but never toppled from a tree just to impress
my mate. Oh let him twitch, gurgle, rant and rave,
plunging into love with great finesse,
and let him filch whatever tricks he must.

Then, like the mocker's mate, I won't resist.

## Blackbird at Easter

First the sound, a shudder
something slipping, toppling
falling in another
room, silent when I enter, settling.

Standing still, I dare
the books to lean, the plants
to quake; I turn my ear
away from work, who breaks

and enters, who shatters peace?
My own blood beats inside blue
walls, my pulse catches, words cease.
The thing's not trying to intrude,

but thrashing to get free.
Slowly I open the stove's iron
doors, the fireless maw, sooty
gritty tunnel to the dawn.

Heat explodes in my face,
feathers splayed in fright
fiercely flung into space,
a black glove shattering light.

A starling lifts and cowers
on a shelf. Out, but still inside.
I open all the windows;
icy wind swirls and guides

the hapless bird back home
to swelling sap and
promises of buds.

# Risen

More dandelions spreading, yellowing up
this lawn, than on any other city plot
I pass in driving home. I slow and stop
just as I have each day since this house caught

fire and burned in autumn wind to ash,
seven children with it. A vacant lot
for years, a patch of fireweed and trash,
then four austere apartment units built

and tenants living there among the crush
and sighs; I see them come and go,
the crackling hiss of fire I can't hush
makes me God over what they do not know.

A child is May ablaze, she's ankle deep
in golden manes, she reaches down,
hands held by once scorched ground, a tongue leaps
up, she tugs a torch of blooms and weaves a crown.

## Moonrise at Chatham Harbor

The moon rises in Boston, too,
sometimes a huge lemon cookie
over Friedman's bakery, turning
on suddenly as a street lamp
on Beacon. Monthly, it takes
our breath away, even there,
even in the city.

But when the moon lifts
out of Nauset Beach, pale,
translucent as a peeled tangerine,
when it rises over low tide
at Chatham Harbor, it is more
than a celestial body over
a city skyline; it rises
out of a form like itself,

released like the papery egg
of the moon snail, shadowy,
inviting as the moon snail itself,
an echo of the globe
from which it rose.

A force we can see into:
how it lures the tides,
how the sphere of it speaks
from behind each phase,
how it heads for its zenith
but never flies too far.

In the city, what do we know
about the moon? It sails up
icy and remote over
the malls and colleges,
between the turrets and the tombs.
Yes, we notice it, before
it's eclipsed by a granite tower,

before some distant rumble
and the trolley comes.

Here, at the harbor,
we grasp with our toes
the tough roots of dune grass.
There is no question of
the hover and power of this moon.
It shakes down light shards
everywhere. Nothing will hide us.
We simply hold out our arms.

## Questions at Kezar Lake

When it is February and dark after long hours
of work, and your dinner is mere intent,
your child is loose in the city and late,
will you remember the sun's slow descent,

a bark softening from the opposite shore,
the last bass boat thrumming home from the brook,
the mist rising from the invisible notch,
and some nameless bird scything the dusk?

When the water has frozen in the pipes,
and your body is rigid with cold and wind,
when the school calls about failing hopes,
will you remember the evening when

the sun pierced by the distant peak
spread like yolk over the Carter Range,
how the lake is the last thing shedding light,
how it rises up with the scent of heat?

Is there a human cell that can hold it all?
I think not: possibly sounds, or some streak
of apricot or purple clouds pressing
over Speckled Mountain, or at midnight

rocking, adrift in the Old Town,
under the brilliant spill of the Milky Way,
pinned by the blaze of Perseids,
chalice of the Pleiades rising in praise.

What if the loons catch us in their net
of spiral laughs, their silver cries?
Gather the sounds as a lens would sight,
then clothed in loon song, be silk
against the winter ice.

## Exploring neighborhoods
*In Sandy's Parish*

At night, we lie out in the humid dark
opening our sight to the vast and arid sky,
let go of daytime vision and the barks

of village dogs, and dive into blackness. I
may know the names of constellations or forget,
but certain nebulae, the twins of Gemini,

a shimmering double or a greenish tint
create a kind of friendly neighborhood.
Like walking home from work, you'd let

habit lead you, familiar stars would
offer pleasure—sudden wedgewood asters.
Why? You know that this one is as old

as the universe, speeding from us or
this has nebulosity and four new stars,
and here, the pale blurs glow in pearly clusters.

Rest on Orion, wander on to reddish Mars.
Silver Saturn floats within its platinum rings.
You're passing hedges, homes and stores.

Not far from Earth, Andromeda spins and flings
her lovely arms, the Dipper draws its arc
and we come home amazed, as if we'd found our wings.

# Trespassing

We're comfortable drinking wine,
doing fine, lying down flat on the asphalt
on the private road to Enclave Point.

At the entrance a guard doesn't want
to let us through, where wild life
takes refuge, where only a few
who were deeded a right to the coast
can pass, but no matter, no skin
off our asses, we simply glide by,
wave at the glowing tip of his
cigarette, we wind between pond
and bay, between expansive mansions,
park near a black meadow
and with binoculars,
                        ride, ride, ride
away from private property,
yeah, we have our spines
on someone's access,
                        but everything
that matters: the spirit, intellect,
soul, have left on Pegasus, high
stepping by each constellation,
two million light years into
our past where Andromeda fans out,
a white talc over the dark
and the trespassing eye is welcome.

# NOT SAILING
*Riding out Hurricane Luiz in Smith's Cove*

Sails furled, sheets coiled, dock lines taut,
cleated, while all around is motion: black seas leap
into blades of silver glinting like stripers, caught.
Flags, banners, wind socks wildly chatter, sweep

and fray. Gulls glide the airstreams, weave their cries,
lead returning boats. Halyards slap into song,
wind churns, erasing the stillness of July,
whistling through the riggings like a flock of swans.

The catboat longs to sail, wind is her siren; she pulls
and lurches at her lines. Perched in fierce sun, astride
her bow, we don't cast off. We jibe and heel
without terror, still at the eye of a wild ride.

# The wind

It might be so still you hear the bees
eating the paint or the loons from far away coves,
and the lake will be oily and flat as our wood stove.
Then, like a train, the wind roars down the valleys,

roughs the lake up like the wrong direction of fur
until it is leaping dolphins and whales in rows
until it is sleek stampeding panthers in droves
until we, in our small boats, are driven to the shore.

Wind inhabits the landscape like a huge beast. Scares
the gray drizzly weather that oppressed us. Breaks
open the sky, lets silver pour over the dark peaks.
Chases the wild things into their lairs.

All this the wind does, air without shape or form,
and we, who can't even see it, feel our bodies hum.

# Closer

I'm probably the last person on earth
to write a poem about a cat, but last night
he slipped inside the sheets, and slept
between us, his legs outstretched to my side,
his head poked into air enough to breathe, and his eyes
wide open, as if he'd been waiting for one of us
to awaken and see him posed like that,
like a child, or a very small furry adult,
nothing like a cat who should be spiraled
inward so his nose is deep in the blond prairie
of his belly and his eyes shut as tightly
as a wound healed over so nothing, not the restlessness
of the bed partners, not the leak of early light
through the blinds, could wake him…instead,
he was wide-eyed staring through me, forcing my eyes open,
not pulling his paw back when I reached out,
using all he had learned when he was not leaping
off the bird cage or flying across the study
skidding through the papers on my desk, when he was not
drinking from the toilet or batting electrical wires
or stalking a moth, in those rare moments of repose,
he'd observed the ways of upright creatures with skin,
and understood the uses of restraint, then
he shed his faux fur and wrapped himself
in the cautious motions of humans, like *long,
long ago, when animals and people lived on earth
and all spoke the same language.*

# Meeting the Birthmother

# Birthmother, a Fantasy at 11

So child, there's a woman you've decided to claim
who deep in her belly and soul knows who you are;
Neither you nor I can know her name.

At times, she stops, wondering who you became;
She who birthed you, remembers and loves you from afar,
her child. There's a woman you've decided to claim

out of whose womb, pink and perfect, you came
to us. You call her Queen or Movie Star.
Neither you nor I can know her name.

And she was young, too young to blame
and fair and blue-eyed like you are
child. This woman you've decided to claim

was much too busy, you say. She had to deal with fame
and you're her princess, you bear the royal scar.
Neither you nor I can know her name.

Radiating like a distant flame,
she pulls you toward her like a star.
Listen, child, the woman you've decided to claim—
Perhaps, someday, we will know her name.

# Her name

Now we are at the edge:
my daughter, 18, legally
on her own, my daughter calling,
writing to find the girl
who birthed her, both girls
finally grown.

I help my daughter draft the letter
to the state where she was born.
They decline. I help her write a letter
to the courthouse where once
in a tiny pink dress, six months after
she was delivered in pink lace, before
she could even walk, the judge reviewed
the papers and pronounced her
ours. And if our letter is convincing,
the judge of Orphan's Court will order
her file, untouched all these years,
opened. And inside

will be a paper with my daughter's name,
and touching that, a paper with another name,
a blood stranger's, a name
with *C*s or *Z*s, *O*s or *I*s, harsh
or musical, we don't have a clue.
Maybe she's changed it, maybe she's moved,
she's a mother again in a new land,
far from the neo-Greek courthouse
on Main street, her name
different from my daughter's,
but one my daughter somehow owns,
a name like stone, secretive,
unmoving, or like a redbird that bursts out
breaking open the gray continuous sky,

and if the clerk of Orphan's Court
can find that woman
and if the woman says "No,
do not release my name" keeping it
private as a healing spell, my daughter
will be given away again, her new light
eclipsed, and if the woman says "Yes"

my daughter will step toward danger
and expectation, toward disappointment
or a dimly possible peace, whichever,
it will never be one daughter, one mother
pale and dark, fighting and loving,
one mother, one daughter. Nothing
so simple, nothing so tense.

# The Letter with No Address

My daughter is writing a letter:
She is moderate, she is reasonable,
she wants to meet in a place away
from her birthmother's home, no one
has to know, no one has to see,
the husband, those other children will never
have to meet, no one has to watch them
in a remote town, in a highway motel
where they peer into a peeled away
mirror staring at their fair skin, their honey hair,
their ample breasts and hips, they lean
closer, their shade and shape an echo,
all these years walking through separate
crowds where no one could compare.
Then sitting on twin beds, backs against red
plastic headboards each dragging on her cigarette,
whispering—as if the deed of reunion were sin—
finding the voice, amazed at a common turn
of phrase, a mirrored gesture,
sorting the questions like piles of socks:
what music they like—that would be important!
what food? what allergies? what clothes gothic
or punk? which holidays, rituals,
which God, men, boys babies abortions adoptions
what kind of work good with the hands, was she
ever in movies? what color eye shadow, blush?
who is the grandma? what country? the father,
his prowess, his picture in uniform? who's died
from what? how many children? where are the cousins?
and did she, the mother, ever dream of this baby
without a name or did she name this baby,
and how did she feel so young, barely teenage herself,
letting a life slip out between thighs, between hands,
a force so powerful, a tide, a tremor that has shaken
the 18 years of my daughter who has baskets of questions,
truckloads, a lifetime of blanks, of question marks falling
out of the sky like a blinding, silencing, heartbreaking snow.

## A Letter Comes

to the birthmother
among the bills and coupons;
what does she know not to open it.
Inside is a question
as unexpected as a first child.
She is the person with the answer.
Her name.
All these years, it was only a name,
functional, bestowed by her mother,
shouted by her friends,
shortened by the truckers
at the stop, her guy, and the girls
at bowling calling across the lanes,
not some big deal—some kid's hope
of a lifetime—not fireworks, not a comet,
not an end or beginning, nothing
she expected to keep hidden in a vault
or reveal in a ceremony—just
two syllables, that's it, circling
her inside and out—just Her, really.
Should she? Should she let
her name be known?

## Meeting the Birthmother

They come toward each other from the edges
of the small park—separated by chestnut trees
and nearly twenty years—Diaspora of the blood.

They walk inward, their breath short, leaning back
toward their pasts, their hearts like cliff swallows
swooping at dusk out of the dark safety of the chest.

They have imagined the other's pale face
without a name—all these years: arms, voice,
hair, a double existing in no fixed place.

Above, maple leaves rustle and hush, rustle and hush.
Starlings weave part of their story in the air.
Their breathing is jagged, comes in a rush

held since the last birth breath, the cry and gasp,
the slipping out and away of the daughter, the first
suck of air into the delicate vase of the lungs.

Everything waits—the two so familiar, so strange
drawn like moths to flame, fly toward opening arms,
gathering strength to shape the other's name.

## First Supper

A woman invites her first and latest child to supper.
She has her daughters run to meet her
at the market down the block.
"You'll know her," and they do—
the mother's double. They bring
lasagna and their sister home.
They are spooning out ricotta,
spreading the noodles with the sauce.
She's rented videos so they can watch
three horror movies in a row,
a clever way to bring a new child in,
letting the kids eat and stare,
not into the eyes of a stranger
but at the tube, glued to the true
terror of night-murder and melting faces,
not the mere arrival of a girl
they never heard of until this month, feeling
safe together against the screams of victims,
the gush of red, the rush of slime,
the torrent of evil mud.
Where is the danger really
in a bit of shared blood?

# What takes its place

Now the myth is bygone,
all that uncertainty and possibility
of the woman of means, the mother
of distant and substantial fame, blond
and glamorous, cruising the corniche in a Porche,
singer inciting riots or a legend of the silver screen;
my daughter could climb out of the womb
of any woman she chose, she could invent
a new form, perfect in every way
except timing and tenacity. But

no. Here is a small blond woman in T-
shirt and jeans, young, purple polish on her nails,
who rises at 6 a.m., ships her other children
off to school and works the truck stop
on Highway 40, a woman the same shape
and size, the same coloring, same nose
and eyes, same tone of voice as my own
daughter's, a woman scarred
with stretch marks and blue veins
willing to own the flesh, to face,
despite the misplaced childhood, the girl she gave
away, to say—*yes, I recognize you: Here are my arms,
my food even, whatever you wish, sisters,
uncles, a grandmother young as your own mom.*
Even though I didn't search, I reach.

# Wedding
*The Green Dress*

*1*

This is the blood, the birth family
of the bride. They want many seats
and all the green dresses. They will reclaim
the girl they gave away. They will glide
through the ceremony as if they'd been,
through all her twenty years,
walking by her side.

*2*

Who slips into the cool length, the green
foliage of the bridesmaid's dress,
who zips it shut, will walk tall
nearly touching the bride,
whatever her failures and strengths.
We want to prepare the bridal path,
flatten the grass, strew petals.
Who leaves behind drudge and ash,
who wears a wreath of tea rose,
carries godetias in bouquets,
that woman, too, is sanctified.
We all know it. We rush to be friend,
to be family, to fit, like Cinderella,
into the green dress.

*3*

When they are actually walking toward the willow,
four bridesmaids on the arms of four ushers,
two by two, I have lost who is in each dress,
flesh of young women, yes, but
whose blood, whose niece, whose friend
is of no consequence, each lovely girl
in her wreath—dark or fair hair in wild curls,
our meadow muses, lithe shapes

from our dreams, a freshness we long for—floats
over the lawn in green, so the bride appears
startling as the first word:
Light.


4

The bride waits in the heartleaves
of lilac, a parent on each arm.
Her father's dazed in his tux on her left;
this girl who cried each time she had to visit
now pulls him close.
Her mother's on her right,
a woman whose hair grayed,
whose teeth ground down during
the adolescence of this child
who pulls her close.

She steps out. The bees are still.
The stream bends toward her.
The willows bow, the linden flickers.
Geese hush and the wind lifts
the orchids wound into the trellis.
Who can see through the eyes of the groom
what light approaches?
Is it blinding? Is it binding?
She walks into the two long arms of her families,
into the forest of green dresses,
flower girls in flowered frocks,
the forms of the formal ushers.

She slips off her shoes, turns
to face her man, her train
curves like a creamy river
about her feet. She is more
than we knew, holding us all
with a gravity like the sun
blazing overhead.

5

I am standing between my lover and my ex-, his wife and baby,
and behind me, the woman who birthed my daughter and her man,
her father and cousins. We are both in pink. Her daughters walk
in the wedding party carrying white baskets of petals. My daughter
is her daughter. I feel myself in these concentric circles
as if my daughter were the pebble dropped and we
were her rings of families held in place by the laws
of the natural world. Guests watch me, look past me
to the woman who matches my daughter in every visible way.
The couple whispers vows. They place their rings. They face
each other holding hands, the singer sings. The wedding circle
sways in the hot sun. Time stops or speeds along, I can't tell which.
All kinds of love, all faiths surge. The minister declares them
man and wife. They stomp on glasses, kiss, and from our wreath
of pinks and greens, from the bower of willows—newly formed, shining,
they emerge.

# Long Distance

# Heirloom

Now dad's words go out like dying stars.
The book says he misunderstands the words.
They enter, twist, reshape themselves,
lovely birds caught in a propeller.

But this same man gave birth to words for me,
names to trees, cadence to blossoms, scent
to the stand of pines, each word awakening
sense, pressed petals of shade and sound.

*Cardinal, tulip, chipmunk, blue jay,*
*aurora, solstice, dragonfly, thunder,*
*evergreen, dogwood, forsythia, forsythia...*
one a whisper, one a chiseled edge of stone.

My father laid each on my tongue
like a crisp wafer of the Savior,
dabbed his palette of wonder
and stroked my world into focus.

Summer Sundays he drove us into hills
where colts leapt in paddocks and deer paused
at the meadow's edge. He unpacked a picnic,
perched me on a split log fence:

post and rail... post and rail... I hooked my legs
into the repetitions, grasped how the border
gives the field its form, its lyric shape,
gives silver grasses intimacy and order.

In the photo, I'm ten in corduroys, hands in
pockets, face squinting and inscrutable, shy,
a gawky knot on a rough bark stanza,
turning my ear to my father's eye.

# Long Distance

I phone
Dad comes when called,
says hello.
I ask him simple things.
*Lunch today?*
I eat, he says.
*Weather today?*
*Did you walk?*

I ask, I chatter. He mumbles, begins
and drifts. His words dissipate. The wind
clatters in the coastal palms. The sea folds
and folds eroding the fragile sand.

I think he has wandered down the hall.
We hold two ends of a jump rope,
an umbilical, but he's put his end down,
lost interest in the day to day that binds families:
a grandchild's grades, her beaus, the weather,
work, health, small talk that stands for feelings.

He is not in.
Not inside. Where then?
Traveling, spinning outward
between the sparse particles,
body still pumping away in Boca,
but mind among dark matter.

*Do not go gentle,* but who is fierce
enough to hold the fading mind?
Larger things call—immense gravity.
The mind, so willful in its day:
passionate, angry, reasoning, warring,
stubborn and longing—suddenly
lets go, chunks of it, gathering loosely
in orbit—an illusion of silver rings
circling an invisible core.

## Lost and found – a story

One day the elevator stops on 2.
Dad's wife gets off, wheels the grocery cart
toward their apartment door expecting
him to follow. But Dad stays on, riding
the 24 floors like a time capsule.
Flo drops the bags, she stops
at every floor, she walks the halls,
she calls the management, she strolls
the lobby, mail room, and garage.
No Dad. Hours pass. Medics come.
Then door to door. Have you seen Mayer,
a man lost in his own building?
up down, lost in thought or
without thought, whose mind once mapped,
rational, has stranded him in a vector of time.
It is late afternoon. He's on 3
in the home of a little lady
just above his own. She opened
when he knocked. Never questioned
that he'd come.  She let him in.
Served up tea. She took her family albums out
and there he was, sipping and turning plastic pages
engrossed as if this family were his own,
as if she'd been waiting for him
to lose his way, as if they both
suddenly came into focus
and were found.

# War Stories

*1*
In the war, my Dad "Wolly" flew
gliders, night missions for a year,
climbed into his WACO, planes of cloth
and banana oil with Lem
or Knute or Leo, Clarence or Les,
in England. Heavy with troops,
supplies and ammunition they were towed
over the channel at dusk, freed
over updrafts of air, invisible
currents, to glide and land—
stealthily as dragonflies, drawn
by a flare, powerless, armed
merely with carbines, Nazis shooting up
through the floor boards—in a narrow zone
near Bastogne, an esophagus
through the enemy's belly. Was that man
any less of a mystery than this one?

*2*
If he wasn't lost, downed
beyond the corridor's boundary,
a flash after enemy fire,
charred flesh and ash,
if in silence, his glider
slipped onto a field
between windrows of cypress,
and troops in camouflage poured out,
then, he made his way back
to the coast, back to his base
in Borham and the empty glider,
flimsey in the Belgian dawn,
poked its hook into the hostile sky
to be caught by an Allied angler
and reeled across the waters
to the proper side. Over and over,
a roulette of fear, a net of death,
a  current of rebirth. So it was
my Dad learned to make his way home.

*3*
Between protective glass and my maple dresser
in my childhood bedroom, was a small photo
of my Dad in uniform, Army Aircorps dress,
a snappy cap, a face so handsome
it broke my heart even before I knew
boys and the twists of beauty, and my Dad,
overseas in action my first two years,
came home to me, one of the few
pilots blessed, possibly by magic glass,
at first, an unwanted stranger
confusing the hierarchy of the home,
then, a Dad, regular, gentle, eager to work.
Whatever fierceness of will had kept him aloft,
seeped into the local hills. Grounded,
he wasn't so lucky. Grounded, he lost
his gift, the wild power to glide.


*4*
When I was a child in the white brick house
on Second Street, my Dad would rummage
through the shelves and bring the dark cracked
violin case downstairs. He'd flick the brass clasps open
and the case, swallowing air, gasped.
We knew my father's past was locked inside,
his stories, everything he saved and savored.
He cupped the gleaming violin, tucked it
under his bruiseless chin, tuned and tuned,
played *Turkey in the Straw* while we stomped around
excited as chickens, and gradually, he fell into
familiar phrases, Bach, Mozart, what did we know?
He was there so close to us,
but gone again to music or to war,
towed into cumulus clouds,
lifted by cadence and spiral columns,
released into risk and passion,
gliding again, oh yes, gliding.

# Caretaking

I learn
the art of seduction,
lead him step
by step toward
the shower, strip
him down until
he's bare—4 p.m.
April 23, 1995, the first
time I have ever seen him naked,
but he is just
a man, narrow hips,
flat buttocks, scrawny thighs,
the penis, the wrinkled testicles,
some wiry hairs,
nothing shocking.
All those modest years
that made him Dad
gone in a wish
for him to shower.
Who am I, some strange
caretaker? Would he let
his daughter peel his
fatherhood away, lead him
to the terror of the shower?
Bravely he steps
over the marble sill.

# Without names

Who is Judy? I tease.
Your dau...I'm giving language hints.
My dad tests the sound: dau...dau...
my dog, he says, pleased.
Ruff, ruff, I say, unbuttoning
his blue striped shirt.

I thought this would make
all the difference, knowing or not
my name, his daughter, but this
is not the case. What is a name?
Sound. Sea in a certain wind. No more
than palm frond clatter. Sometimes

he utters my name;
it glides through like a gull,
or he mutters Anne or Fay
his dead sisters, or Flo, his wife.
And the word "daughter?"
a flimsy stutter for the real

thing. He holds my hand, lets me
guide him, waits for me, hugs me.
Stripped of phonetics, of formality,
of definition, we are pure
photon, our love beaming
from cell to cell.

# Barely holding

We are at the lip of the sea,
froth at our feet.
Stay here, I tell my Dad
and I run for beach chairs,
run backwards, facing the waves,
toes dancing in the hot sand.
My father takes a step forward
bending into the constant wind,
he leans against the blue horizon
on the edge of balance—still
as a marble discus thrower
who has already
let go.

◆

We sit in our plastic beach chairs
the tide approaching our toes.
Rush crash rush crash
no need for speech
the wind swallows our sound.
My father is too bent
to follow boats, the ships of clouds.
We focus on the glitter, the shine,
of jingle shells; small birds
peck and skitter at our feet.
Bit by bit, the sea surrounds,
our feet submerge,
our chair legs sink,
slowly, slowly,
we are losing ground.

# April 15, 1996

7 a.m.: the sun rises huge out of the Atlantic behind the nurse arriving
    to check my father's breathing.
From the front door, you can hear my father rasping, frail as tinder
    in his complex bed,
his chest and neck, belly heave behind each breath. I hold *my* breath
    to hear *his*. Even
his bed breathes more easily than he does. The mattress inhales, exhales,
    sighs. I step outside
and look East. I am deafened by breathing. Mine are long swells breaking; his
    are whitecaps, sharp and shallow.
The sea breathes, you can count on it. Even after, when there is dead
    silence in the bedroom facing West,
the sea takes up his rise and fall, without grieving, day and night, living
    through his leaving.

## April 16, 1996

This day, hawks in great numbers
spiral up the coast over the ordinary gulls
and cries of terns, above the fleet of pelicans
grazing the condo towers. Hawks
rise on salty thermals, released
from the glint of perch, the flack and spatter
of surf; their fringed wings, as wide
as the afterlife, barely finger the wind.
A body is draped in green and wheeled
away, while loops of hawks soar
and glide, ascending.

# Waning
*at Penobscot Bay, July 16, 1996*

Yesterday the sky closed down,
sea closed in, color blinked out.
Particles of grey fog crept
over lichen, through lupine
and porchrail veiling his spark.

My father's eyes were ocean,
sky the way you see it from
this point, open, tented on
poles of spruce. His eyes held light
as sea does, or did until

he died, his form receding.
We drew the tissue flesh of
eyelids down and darkened blue,
darkened day, the ebb and flow,
the lunar wink, solar glow.

Dawn today, our cataracts
dissolve, blue yolk of sea is
whole again, and all it holds
is ours, its singing can be
seen. Blue weaves through evergreen.

# Endangered

I need to see fireflies, their honeydew light,
their unexpected constellations. Blinking
out notes and intervals in our side yard
on June nights, they wove a score around
my father, a polyphony of sparks.

Now, each dusk, I'm in pursuit
wishing to be caught in their pale flight,
drawn back to my father's glow in his garden.
But fireflies have left town, and night congeals,
heavy, uninterrupted on our urban lawns.

At the edge of Hammond and Jamaica Ponds,
at Hall's, the Muddy River, nothing flickers
among the cattails and the weeds. My father,
so recently extinguished, leaves behind
an uncharmed darkness. Waiting

to read his signal, I dissolve
in shadow under a canopy of beech.
I brush my hands over foliage,
reaching for a fragment of his heat.

# The Art of Granddaughters

# Birthday poem for cheyenne rose

Your mother was a girl with a history:
punk, tattoo, drop-out, runaway,
but now she has made you
and inside you swim and tumble,
grow nubs and brows
elbows and fingernails.
Tethered in your tiny space
you send out signals of creation
a jab, a kick, a hiccup
and around you
like a galaxy that's newly formed,
your mother spins too.
Leaving her wild disorder behind,
she comes into focus,
and in your room-to-be
she sets up crib, pillows,
little booties, creams and powders,
red mittens small as rose petals.
Curtains that match.
Worn and fresh books in stacks,
tapes of lullabies next to
Guns and Roses.
Not even fully formed,
you make a quiet revolution
from inside. This is before
the violent pain. Your mother is ready
for that too. Her screams will
become your first breath,
and your first breath will change
everything.

## POEM FOR MY DAUGHTER
*December 25, 1994*

You called us from the Labor Suite.
Sweet labor.
Christmas eve.
They put you in a room with a phone,
your husband pressing his strength
into your hand. We, on our extensions,
a thousand miles away counting
with you. You, breathing and counting,
gasping and laughing
after all that false labor,
joyous with relief,
finally something true.
The baby is done.
Ready to see the light.
And you, my darling, ready to give.
*Dar a luz.* To give to light.
We thought we'd give birth with you
on the line, but we were sleeping
through the hours of the night
your body was contracting
contracting without success
and in the pre-dawn of Christmas day,
the masked team sliced
your belly for the treasure,
lifting your perfect baby
into the glare of the surgical lights:
the down, the silky hair, wrinkled fingers,
feet folded up along the legs
like wings really, slits of eyes,
little ears with rims and vortices,
tender lips, smooth rosy gums,
the bud of a tongue, a voice,
veins, blood, heart, lungs,
all of it pressed against your worn out
thumping chest, your collapsing womb.
Her precious face; a child is born,
is given.

# GENDER

They told you, probably a boy,
shadows on the sonograms.
You gave up your dreams:
little girl dresses,
little girl dolls.
We picked out pale green quilts,
yellow sleepers, bright blue pants.
Good, I said. Non-sexist buying.
Untempted by frills.
Then out of the womb,
they lifted the child, hmmmm, they said
behind the curtain that hid the blood,
looks like it might be a girl,
a what!
maybe a girl
a girl?
it *is* a girl, look
a girl
and you wept,
not for the wound in the body,
not for the glow of the child,
not for the end of squashed organs
and a shortness of breath, the hard
work of the birth, no, you wept
for the girlchild you longed for,
all you ever wanted, something of
your own body, to hold
in your arms day after day.
A girl! you grinned when you woke.
A girl! the next morning in disbelief.
A girl! taking her to the breast.
I left you suckling her,
bought four pink outfits,
two with bows, oh God,
how quickly the dogma slides
away.

## BERRY PIE, OH CHEYENNE
*A Grandmother's Song*

Do you like my berry pie?
Filled with berries blue as sky
Do you like my berry pie?
Sweet wild berries
Sweet child, hurry!
Sweet juice, very berry pie.
    Come and see what's in my pan.
    Come and taste it, oh, Cheyenne!

Do you like my forest pie?
Moss and starwort piled up high.
Do you like my forest pie?
Lichen ruffles
Pine cone truffles
Sappy needles, forest pie.
    Come and see what's in my pan.
    Come and smell it, oh, Cheyenne!

Do you like my lily pie?
Green and creamy lily pie.
Do you like my lily pie?
Water flowers,
Long stemmed ovals,
Froggy floaters, lily pie.
    Come and see what's in my pan.
    Come and touch it, oh, Cheyenne!

Do you like my pebble pie?
Speckled pebbles, smooth and dry.
Do you like my pebble pie?
Quartz and granite,
Geode planets,
Mica, sandstone pebble pie.
    Come and see what's in my pan.
    Come and grasp them, oh, Cheyenne!

Do you like my ocean pie?
Full of roars and leaps and sighs.
Do you like my ocean pie?
Seaweed swishes,
Jellyfishes,
So delicious, ocean pie.
    Come and see what's in my pan.
    Come and listen, oh, Cheyenne!

Do you like my meadow pie?
Pretty monarch butterfly.
Do you like my meadow pie?
Green grasshoppers,
Buttercuppers,
Picnic suppers, meadow pie.
    Come and see what grandma's planned.
    Hugs and kisses for Cheyenne!

# Thanksgiving Ritual

Cheyenne, almost four, sets the table, learns
to place the knives to the right of the plates,
and they are there, askew like pick-up sticks,
their handles distant, their blades easily grabbed,
then the spoons, doing better, oval faces
generally peering up, and forks plunked
on linen napkins to the left of plates. Here my
mother slips from heaven with advice,
and her mother, corrects in a heavy accent;
after all, it's her silver, her china,
her lace cloth. Undaunted

by the ancestors' guiding hands,
Cheyenne reinvents tradition, takes
from her toy kitchen plastic food, running
between rooms to set one piece on each plate,
vile purple grapes, a wan banana, a wedge
of yellow cheese, two weiners
attached at their midriffs, and something
we guess is macaroni.

"Gram," she exclaims,
even as I set another steaming bowl,
"I'm running out of food!"
Confident as Martha Stewart, she places
one polyurethane kitty from her Pet Shop
by each wine glass, and one Lego
as a garnish for the vinyl food. Now
she leads our guests toward her work of art
pressing us where she wants us each to sit.

Over such gifts, real and imagined, fragrant and inert,
we give thanks, and for the hands and vision
of Cheyenne, we are uncommonly blessed.

# The art of granddaughters

I mail them pens,
paint, stamps and inkpads,
lovely papers. What
am I thinking?
I, a distant grandma,
picture neat block letters
of names and bright
yellow ducks in a row, as if
the plump arms wielding
the rubber stamps
were robots'; I even hope for
alien heads and stick bodies,
hair like pins, and the swash
of gooey color from a brush,
red sky purple trees a gash
of thick thick black, yes creative, but
all within the confines of the page.

No way, grandma—the tool
connects the mind to the world,
drawing from it, drawing on it:
a border of glue on the kitchen
table, flight of blue butterflies
on the bathroom wall, (after all
roses bloom in perfect repetitions
at the ceiling's edge), plant
spatters of acrylic green
over the hardwood floor,
and odd creatures etched
under flickers of the bedroom lamp.

My girls are not the first
to sample surfaces, to choose

the rise in the nylon rug
for the hump of a dino,
to dot raindrops
on the window glass,
to fresco swirled plaster
into mermaid's sea,
bump brush over
couch covers, press pen

into the grain of pine,
mix ochre and cereal
to sign, as the ancients did,
their palm prints
on the glistening walls.

## Check-up
*for Cheyenne, at four*

Even though we have peered in each others' ears with the plastic light and listened to each others' hearts, taken deep breaths and tweezed out splinters with the doctor's kit, even though we have switched roles twenty times and healed and tortured dolls and yelled *no, no, not the shot!* in the voice of Cuddles the stuffed bear and Zodi the real and hyper dog, we must do it again, *once more* you say, *once more... you be the doctor, then once more me...well, really once you me you me*....I shake my head (already examined to death). Once! I say and stick out my tongue for the depresser, clutching my throat, croaking with strep; and before this, we are playing "food" with plastic eggplants and watermelons on a plastic grill, and after, we will play "house" with Lego children and Playskool cars, children who will lie down and be dead, and a mother who slides into a trash bin from her porch; on the kitchen floor we race model cars that wind back into their wheels and sprint forward across linoleum to crash into stenciled walls, and from the crack of dawn when Cheyenne raises her tender lids and stands over me saying, *Gram, I'm starting to get up,* we cut and paste yellow chimneys onto blue houses, we draw windows and cut them open, blinded by light, we use our glue sticks as if the neighborhood would fly apart without us, we press glinting stickers onto our art and foreheads and palms, onto the plants and the dog's wet snout, then draw umbrellas since it's "U" Show and Tell at day care and all Umbrellas are lost; *no Underwear*, Miss Patty warned, allowed as an artifact of "U"; we must read *Swimmy* and discuss the Bad Tuna, and as busy as we are, the dog, who is newly acquired and only six months in this world, is tearing about the house, leaping onto the couch, chewing every toy, vacuum part, phone wire and pillow. Where are the parents who so reasonably left their child for only an hour? Night has come, cars grind up the steep suburban hills, but no one rattles to a halt, except me, old Gram, worn out by plastic and imagination. Cheyenne does not wind down like a metal car, she is pounding the reflex hammer on my kneecap, taking the blood pressure of my toes, *that's enough nap, Gram, up up, you be the doctor now, ask me again, ask me how I feel.*

# DIRECTIVE

When Cheyenne disappears
when she needs to run
to tear that seam between you
won't spare your tears,
if she has your restless gene
that drew you to trolleys, made you
ache for trains, slip away to other towns
looking for refuge, then you put her
on the bus with some bucks to Boston;
call me, tell me the time
she'll arrive. I'll be there for
the lithe runaway with long red hair,
the little mermaid swimming for freedom;
don't let her wander the West Virginia hills,
the abandoned strip mines, don't let her
stagger up the slagheaps of Pennsylvania or ride
the bland Ohio highways with a boy in black leather,
let her step off into my arms to hide, I'll tell you nothing
after "she's safely arrived," all secret from then on, out
of harms way; that's what I'm here for: aging, changing
the sheets, hanging up sweet curtains, waiting for her bus.

# First time

I have never had, always made a point of not having, a fir tree at Christmas. Growing up as a conservative Jew in a small working class Catholic town, I felt different. My parents encouraged that. In kindergarten, I refused to make Christmas cards. This was 1948 long before anyone considered "celebrating diversity." Ms. Wallace called my mother to report my insubordination. My mother enlightened her as to the possibilities of Chanukah cards. I did not mutter the required Lord's prayer each morning at school and this resistance ensured that every word is indelibly engraved on the gray matter of my aging brain.

    I carried my grandmother's graceful weighty menorah both into and out of my marriage and it still flickers meaningfully, brass and fire, dull and satiny to honor violence and miracle in my kitchen. But this year, my fifty-sixth, I entice my daughter (who has unaccountably become Christian) to come visit with my granddaughter for the Christmas holiday. She won't fly; she must drive for two days in winter to come to Boston. I say I will have Christmas if she comes. This is how badly I long to see my grandchild. To my amazement, my daughter accepts. My fate is sealed. I commence interviewing Christian friends about the subtleties of buying a tree. Shake it. Test the tenacity of its needles. Consider its shape, density, softness. Have them slice off the bottom. Then water and water.

    For two weeks I can't sleep. Little questions nag at 2 a.m. A holder, the lights, I do not have even one golden ball, one miniature sleigh, and so it begins. I wander into the ethnic stores first, buy paper maché deer, raffia lions, cloisonné balls, nothing that reeks of religion, not one angel, not even a conical Claus. I stick to the pagan—creatures, flowers, stars. Whoever is watching can't distinguish me from a nature study guide. But I disintegrate quickly. Within a week, I am walking through the aisles of a full-fledged Christmas store, scrutinizing pearly glass balls, and strands of satin and velvet. A leaded clear glass angel calls to me. Think, who saved Isaac from the knife? I tuck the delicate angel into my basket among icicles and strings of lights. At home, my stash is growing on the dining room sideboard, and still no tree.

    I pick the day, the place, no disreputable heap of Trees for Sale parking lot tucked between two city warehouses. A nursery in the Western suburbs. I pass it on my way to work. It is a chilly day, December 10th, but I am sweating. I pretend I am there to look around. I case the inside first, lured by wreaths and fragrant bundles of fir, then scout the lot. I glance upward furtively, waiting for lightning to strike. There are hundreds of trees. I approach a guy leaning against the shed. "I need your help," I say. He slowly stands up straight. "This is my first time."

He shows me many nicely shaped balsam firs. I don't need to shake them to see they are already shedding needles. And this is the reputable place. I stand in front of one after another, expressionless. I should have brought a Christian.

"When I take it home, can I keep it outside for a week?"
"Sure, it's a tree. Put it in a bucket of water right away."
"What if it turns cold?"
"It's a tree. It came from a forest."
"What if the water in the bucket freezes?"
"It won't be able to drink it then, will it?"

He lets on that there is a more expensive alternative; the Fraser Fir holds on to its needles longer. He shows me three. He says this is the kind he buys. Why not? If it's only this one Christmas tree this one time, then let's have the Bloomingdales of Christmas trees. I pull my hand along a branch. Those needles stick on like a porcupine's. Yeah, it's a little bushy around one side of the bottom. It's top mast lists to the left. But, he almost promises, it will stick together until December 25th. I buy it. He wheels it off on his gurney to the operating table where the bottom of its trunk is severed. He pulls a red and white net around it as if dressing a model in a skin-tight sheath. He loads it onto my roof rack. I thank him more profusely than seems reasonable, pay a bundle, gather my cache of ornaments and the large plastic tree stand and head back to Brookline.

I stop twice, once on Route 128 and once on the Turnpike, to check the tie-downs. The minute I leave Brighton and enter Brookline, I begin to worry. You can't hide a tree riding on top of your car even it's wrapped in a hair net. I turn onto my street. Shall I park in front of someone else's house? But then how will I lug it to mine? I stand on the sidewalk between my car and my porch. Orthodox men are walking past me towards late afternoon services at the *schul* on the corner of my street. They know me, although they never acknowledge me. In winter, I wear slacks; in summer, I wear shorts. But this will clinch their disdain.

I go inside and get a knife. I come out and make sure no one is coming. My neighbor pulls out of her driveway, but heads in the direction away from my house. I cut the jute rope that holds the tree to

my roof rack. I tug it toward me. It rolls onto me with a fragrance I want to die in. It is too heavy for me to lift, so I grasp the trunk end and drag it up my front steps to a corner of my porch. Its fishnet stocking holds it together. I am not yet ready to bring it into my house. Now I grunt and moan and lift it into the green plastic tree holder. I tighten one screw and the tree slumps toward the porch rail. I run around it, lift it and tighten the opposite screw. It's sort of upright. I work in the last two screws. It's not exactly vertical, but it's the best I can do on my own.
I go inside and fill my watering can. I pour water into the base and can almost hear the tree suck it up. I return to the street and stare back at the house to see if passersby will notice that I have a Christmas tree on my porch. It's not too visible. You could mistake it for a hanging potted evergreen if you were very nearsighted.

Inside, I lay out my ornaments on the dining table. They are a mishmash of materials. Primitive and factory made. Is there a theme here? I seem to have lost sight of my pagan beginnings. I will wait for my granddaughter to decorate the tree.

I leave the tree on the porch five days and nights. I leave its net on for the first two days to help it survive a wind storm. I visit it frequently and water it twice a day. I speak to my granddaughter long distance. "Gram, do you have the tree set up?" " It's here," I say, relieved to have done the deed. On December 14th, the man who shovels my snow comes by. He asks me why my tree is on my porch. I have trouble explaining this. He asks why I have a tree? He asks if I want help bringing it inside. Without dwelling on it, I say yes. I move a chair, a lamp. I know where it is going to go. We tip the whole tree over, pour the water out of the plastic base and lug it inside. My God, the tree is here right in my wide front hall, deep green and spreading its thick scent. When you open the front door, the tree will be the first thing you see.

Now I am living with someone. I fix some dinner. I sit by the tree and eat and smell the fir. I stroll by my decorations. Just one or two, I think. I choose two animals and bring them to the tree. I hang each on a branch. Try different branches. Make adjustments, stand back. I gather a few more and hang them. I drape the satin ropes, the golden chain. I hang the, oh yes, pearly balls. And last, what should have been first, the tiny twinkly lights. At 10 p.m. I plug it in. There is a vague rumble under the floor. Just the distant trolley shaking the neighborhood. Then it's perfectly quiet. Perfectly shocking and beautiful.

"Gram," says my granddaughter, who was lifted from my daughter's womb Christmas morning, "we have to go to bed early so Santa Claus will come." I see there's more to this than a balsam fir. Now I'm a goner. I buy a red velvet stocking with gold trim. I buy a pack of candy canes. I buy a hand painted Santa ornament. It's all I can do to turn away from the crèches.  Someone is going to have to pretend to come down the chimney. Who will this be?

# Departure

They left an hour ago, their van loaded with bags and gifts: my daughter, her boyfriend, and my granddaughter with whom I have just spent ten days and nights of unmitigated delight. On Christmas eve, my granddaughter Cheyenne still put up four fingers when asked her age, but on Christmas morning she looked at her hand with new awe, wiggled each finger and a thumb and pressed her whole palm out into the air. Five. And the world was hers. Learning the route to the trolley stop, testing the ride sitting forward and backward or forward twisted backward, moving toward the front so she could determine which lever on the driver's panel controlled the trolley door, she was five. Exploring the elaborate climbing structure at the Children's Museum, racing up the ramps to keep up with the sharks and sea turtles in the Aquarium's tank, mesmerized by the sea lions who bark, kiss and do ballet, she was five. That was great, she said, hopping down the metal stairway. Great, she said skipping through the penguin-filled lobby, great, great, great—rising a little more with each step as if gravity affected her less than other humans. Fabulous, she escalated.

And that was before the full moon rose, significantly brighter than any time in the last century. We sat in a window sill recess on the ninth floor of City Hall and watched it lift out of Boston Harbor, huge, orange and so ripe its edges threatened to spill over onto the airport and the glowing towers. Quincy Market glittered with holiday lights and the trees wrapped with bulbs twinkled madly in the wind. "A light woods," Cheyenne declared, and finding it hard to believe that the moon would rise up high in the sky and turn silver, she invented a game where she looked away (down at the street or toward an inside corridor) and then back at the moon, gasping with surprise each time, acknowledging its tiny movements upward. We found that same moon, much higher, much whiter, when we stepped off the trolley at Washington Square. Great, she muttered, her energy waning momentarily.

Late late at night, after dancing in tutus, several *Frog and Toad* stories and the unavoidable *Lion King 1*, her eyes close on the last phrase of Langston Hughes' poem *April Rain Song*, "and I love the rain." Boom. She's out until morning when she stirs, flings her arms wide, sleeps, stirs and flutters her eyes open. She wobbles out of bed in her long pink Barbie nightgown, smiling, ready to receive the world.

Thirty six pounds including her new sneakers that blink and velvet pants, and in that compact body is the capacity to discuss, analyze, reflect, dispense compassion, and express her feelings. I love you, she offers freely. You are my sunshine, she sings. At the Puppet Showplace she sits enthralled, repeating every line the puppeteer directs us to. So focused, she's barely breathing. At home, we set up our own puppet theatre and perform extemporaneously with our home-made puppets which keep losing eyes or hair. We glue as we go. We have a king, a queen, a dragon, a witch, of course, but also Pegasus, who drags the sun into the sky and saves everyone by melting one enemy after another. Before we can go to bed, we must drive around town and check out the Christmas lights in Brighton and along the Commonwealth Mall and colorful Commons, but it is Newbury Street with its glitter and sophistication that woos her. Maybe when you grow up and become a lawyer or veterinarian, you'll come and shop here. No, she says. I don't want to be a lawyer. I'm going to be a princess.

They call twice before they reach the turnpike to report things they've left behind. I strip the beds, clean up stray ribbons and the crumbs from her birthday celebration, I remove clay snakes from the breadbox and crayons from the bathtub. I gather the scraps of paper that remind me what I haven't done in ten days. I can't remember how I actually raised children and went to work. Miraculously, I make five phone calls in a row. I type an invoice with no one on my lap. No little fingers trying to usurp my keyboard. Things suddenly become too simple. The little bird slipped on her pink parka, the pink princess, laser of joy, and flew. The world recedes a bit, pales to winter grays.

# LONG DISTANCE WITH CHEYENNE

Sometimes she just breathes deeply
on her end of the phone or hums
or drawls—after your many questions, sleepily—
some non-sequitor like "Gram,

I have new daisy sandals." She can't wait
to take the phone, but then she listens
as if she kind of smells and tastes
your longed-for voice through distance.

She's close to you, in your ear, smiling,
"Gram, I wish you would come over
here, I haven't seen you in a couple of whiles."
Then maybe you're saying you love her

and she blurts out "Bye," a sudden gust on water.
Her present lassoes her. She's gone. Granddaughter.

# Working on Words

## What becomes of poems

From a sound, maybe, foam at the riverbend,
a downed tree, a scarf of black birds,
the poem begins its first life
as a praise or a record.
It is made for that moment
wrapped in its stiff bark of meaning,
a decent poem; the listener breathes with it
and something sharpens.

Yet the pulp of it and the sap
thicken inside its foliage of words
with a cadence of lullabies,
childhood's clatter and scents,
names of sisters or pets.

And one day a child is born,
a parent dies, vows are taken
or broken and the poem breaks
into flower, wild apple or huge
chestnut candles, blazing away now,
illuminating like a nova,
splitting the daytime sky.

# Your old notes
*for Robin*

At this late age, I study modern poems
using your old green book
*Eliot: Complete Poems and Plays*
loose in its spine,
its cloth mottled and smooth
from your youthful hands,
and inside, your name,
and '63, your senior year at Brown.
Engulfing the poems, your tidy notes
in blue ball point slant from the text
out toward the edges like rays
from the burning words;
your script weaves in through the type
among the thoughts and guts of Eliot,
your thoughts, or rather those of Hyatt Waggoner
lecturing a stream of lucid discourse on the poem
sieved through your mind,
your mind recasting his
mining the mind of the poet.
Studying the page,
I am looking back through time
as we do peering into the universe.
Long before I knew you,
before we pored over poems together,
you made these notes unknowingly
for me who would, some thirty years later,
using your old text, make a crosshatch
of commentary, my notes perpendicular
to yours, Vendler and Waggoner sparking
across a generation, and all of us packed
between the boards, pressed into and by Eliot
whose lines rise up and out of our labyrinth
to mystify and shine.

# Work

Work is what gets done
without distraction,
but without distraction,
what fills the work,
what pulp, what meat,
what bittersweet?
Work is simply an outline,
a shadow, a gesture
without meaning.
Work is posture;
distraction is leaning.
Distraction tugs at the heart,
it shoots you up with guilt
or passion, it makes you wait,
it's tension, it's traction,
stretching the mind out,
keeping you straight.

## "Are you mumbling to yourself"

my son says, stumbling
on some utterance. Driving,
searching for books, filling in forms,
shopping for dinner, scribbling poems,
words escape like caged doves
surprising even me
with their disturbing moans.

My mother talked to herself, a running list
of chores—aloud—repeated as she headed
toward straightening the drawers,
and when she wrote a check or letters,
she was a distant freeway of cars,
rumbling. I suspected she had crazy times,
anger that made her slam the doors;
I thought her mumbling was a sign.
Before she died, she muttered
numbers and incomprehensible names,
syllables thrumming as a final rain.

I told myself: I will never be
like her and yet the words
leak out as if I cannot seal my seams.

Who am I to keep words safe
      as if I were a vault?
            Let them out!
I like their taste
      their shape and sharpness,
           their chartreuse softness.

Below the surface, they are silent
      shadows cast by reefs of thought,
         but free in air, words
             release like rubbed leaves of
               raspberries
       basil
              mint.

# Waiting for the Word to Come

What I'm talking about
is the way a person,
a child even, pauses
in mid-speech and waits
for the right word,
glazed suddenly
in the face, while
inside, that person
watches for a word
to surface like a rock
from the cold packed
garden into light,
or you can almost
feel the child let
down a wooden bucket
into a deep well
hoping the much needed
word lurks beneath
black water, and the arm
makes a gesture like
cranking or grasping
for fireflies, and
suddenly, it's there:
silver water, a pewter fish,
a pale green beacon
slipped into the sentence
which hovered in air;
the word, when spoken,
flits out blinking and dipping
inscribing itself
on the listening dark.

# Defining

The leaves are not a flaming torch
   leading the way into the darkest months,
are not autumn's last blazing breath.
   In fact, they are cool to the touch.

They are simply their name—red maple;
   not the raw palms of pilgrims in prayer,
the enemy extinguished by napalm,
   not my mother's death, not passion's flare.

Still moist, traced with gnawing and veins,
   in the absence of deep summer green
and before the late October rains,
   they are finally scarlet, finally what they mean.

# A MOMENT IN EVERY CLASS

There is a moment in every class when the subject has been circled,
or flown like a banner or chewed, and the poems read and swallowed
or maybe held in the cheek like spinach, the instructions printed clearly
on the board where the kids are not looking, which might be out the window
or into their desks or themselves, a moment when I ask myself what
am I doing here, when my age suddenly claims my body which was,
all these years, leaning toward the children as if I were the only muse
they had. Fatigue breaks in a wave over me, weights me down, even my
vision scatters like still water broken by rising carp. Children flutter up
from the floor, there is noise, wings of many large birds clattering; they settle
at desks and hunch over blank paper, frail yellow paper, nothing enticing
enough to call out the poem. It seems no word, not one, will crease
the desert of the page; some children fuss over pencils, others wave their
hands toward me as if I were a well of language they could tap, but am I?
I wish I could hand them bouquets of phrases, but they must pick their own
from a landscape only they wander. One by one they start down the path,
leaving their desk mates behind,  listening for bluejays or the exact way wind
ruffles the maple, scraping against the bark of elm, the harsh façade
of the alley. Now there is a muttering from within, words whispered and
written, cadence and breath, meaning and the awe of where the poem
is leading. The real muse, hanging back in the doorway until it feels welcome,
drifts down the aisles, slipping from shoulder to shoulder, speaking its
invisible words into the ears of those who will listen. Now children circle me,
in love with their own voices, eager to put their poems into air, rose balloons,
cumulus clouds, weather to be reckoned with, and I am shaken once more
by the act of language, by the fact that words quiver the mouth, tighten
the knot at the base of the throat, quicken the pulse, that what is crafted
and spoken on tentative breath has the force of flood, can change the course
of feeling; so it is hard to turn away, even when the body has had enough,
the spirit longs to hear the poem inside the child.

# Every poem is an emergency

The child has finally written the poem
she cannot write. She runs
to the woman whom she knows
will know what she has done
but the woman is somewhere
else and the child cannot
just leave the poem
on the woman's desk
or simply wait until tomorrow,
the poem must be given
from the child's hot hand
into the woman's. Inside
her body there are sirens
and flashing lights, adrenaline
courses, her pulse accelerates.
This is a matter of life.
The poem, once written,
must be given
now.

## Bringing with me

I stroke and feather marking the slate of lake,
slicing ripples, drawing out the light,
black silhouette of loon, dark swoop of hawk,
mountains from the vestiges of night.

My kayak slips along the lily path,
The shoreline birches bend to sip the sky,
green pads, green palms, cream blooms are scything past
and on the universe, I am dragonfly.

From the headphones tight against my ears,
city children hesitate and speak
in low, shy voices difficult to hear.
I drift and listen hard: "A man with teeth

as cold as ice, without a home;" "orchards
of lonely women shriveling in sun;"
"words, harsh and tortured stones." These poems
rise up from students who can stun,

who  murmur inside me now, their terrain
sharp inside the one I'm gliding through.
They will not hear the kingfisher's refrain
or marvel at the peaks within my view,

but they have caught me with the lean and sway
of voices rooted deep inside the mud.
I dip into both worlds, swirling the clay.
Tangled, then released by weeds and words.

## Advice at the Mill River

Just stay here. You have a fan. You have a lamp.
The tide runs out from under your porch
and the dock lies down in the mud.
You have paper, a pen, a candle.
Fresh corn, a piece of fish. The sun
is a flume of fire falling into the shrinking river.
The view will not be better at the beach.
You have seen the ledges, their pools and beards
and the village is predictable and small.
Be still. All year you longed for this,
sent children out on their own, dispatched
the troubles of adolescence, farmed out
the warbling canary, the final goldfish
who will not die, freed the hamster in a city park.
Your students have gone off and you
have changed them or you have not.
Do not flee in your car. Observe.
A gull slides across a channel, a deep place.
With a reverent silence, the landscape
becomes new every moment. Tonight,
your porch lamp will glow across the mud.
Stay awake. Witness this.
From somewhere in Ipswich Bay, an entire river
of water will fill this emptiness, like dreams do
the sleeping mind, flooding shoreline marshes,
rock crevices, reaching under your
precarious shack, briefly, completely.

## June at last

It is June at last,
the sun shines, a wind
whips the shirts
the neighbor pins
on her line,
her long blond
hair radiates
the dappled light,
the colors of cloth
blossom in a garden
row, lemon and scarlet
aqua and rose,
and the white
white of her baby's
clothes. My neighbor
works outside
in the glorious day
like my mother
used to,
while I'm inside
praising the prints
of pajamas,
the smack of wet
clean sheets,
stretching my own
cotton line
and putting up
poems.

## Sous la causse
*Dordogne, France*

1   The Naming

Under the rolling causse, its back
a fur of corn and walnut groves,
under the mild plodding of cows,
the fox strolling the furrows,

are leaping, running, fighting, flying creatures,
fish chiseled with knapped flint on limestone,
pairs, herds, friezes high on the ceilings
of caves, low on the muscled walls, sketched
in charcoal, painted in ochre, scrawled bison,
deer, goats, ibex, rhinoceros and woolly mammoth,
panthers, lions, fantastic antlers, heavy haunches,
fragile legs, delicate muzzles, horns like bolts of lightning,
holy creatures of the hunt.

Lascaux, Pech-Merle, Font de Gaume, Rouffignac,
Les Combarelles, the sacred names of ancient grottos.


2   The Maker

He watches for color, for brush fur and feathers.
Gathers kaolin by chalky cliffs,
and under the lip of the hill,
ochres: red, brown, gold,
charcoal after fire embers die,
colors wrapped in skins, slung over shoulder.

He grinds color, blends it with marrow fat,
blood, urine or sap, tilts fire
to a pool of oil, clears
the secret opening, bends into it,
supplies tied carefully, slides
into a darkness so total, only a bite
of cavern opens to his torch. Seasons,
cycles, forward time, suddenly halt.

He feels along the rocks, holds his lamp aloft.
Where in the wall's topography
do the animals dwell?  Here is the hint
of a snout, trunk of a mammoth, alert turn
of an ear, flying mane in a natural calcium stain.
He crouches to prepare his palette
or builds a scaffold, climbing toward a dome
to lie like no one live has ever done.

For days, he's buried with the muse
fasting, wrapped in darkness, he invents
motion, depth, shading, withholds
paint to indicate a joint. A horse gallops
from his mind, trailing spots
that form an aura around its head.
Beasts gather, fur glistening, sleek.
He ensures the herds and swarms,
evokes their tread.


3   The Guide
*Les Combarelles/ Les Eyzies*

Maybe he walks up the road from the farm
to his job, turns into the grassy lot, crosses
the narrow stream, the field of yarrow,
climbs up through evergreen,
up the causse on the spongy path,
to approach to unlock to enter
a bank of earth through an old iron door.
Or maybe he lives inside
that earthen mouth in total darkness
and creaks the iron door open at
appointed times, squinting
as if daylight or seasons,
visitors for that matter, or this millennium
were mysteries beyond his comprehension.

The important caves sold out,
we, desolate, gladly directed to this lesser cave,
followed the only path, trekked uphill;
blocked, we stood gaping, unsure as young explorers,
pounded on the heavy door, calling for the troll,
sat down in the worn soil.
A crack, a leak of icy breath,
the little man with his lamp croaked to us,
"Pas maintenant. Revenez à midi."
Clank. The cavern sealed again.
The wrap of summer heat.

By noon, twenty have gathered. The guide
opens the door enough to let us through;
he leads us to the center of the grotto room,
slouches back to slam the door. That
is the last of light, of summer's warmth.
Now he has us! It's more authentic
than I'd bargained for. The shock of burial
takes my breath; I sag. My friends close in,
lend me air and pulse. Our guide holds

his meager light against the stone.
It glistens, wakes again for him; he mutters,
"ces empreintes de burin, ces teintres d'ocre,
ces croupes et ces crinières..."
I peer, aching for prehistory. He coos
and whispers, illuminates too briefly. This
is his cave, his world, he gives and takes away.
Can we see with his eye, he who has twisted through
tunnels since the first one? Bend here,
he motions; we bow under a lip of stone,
the wolf's snout, the mammoth's trunk.
I think I see them, straining as I do for galaxies,
eager to believe.

4   Palimpsest
*Lascaux*

Relief, overlap, overlay, a deer leaps out of the ribs
of the bull, fish flip in the flank, ibex twists out of taurus.
The awed next artist three thousand years after the first,
strokes ochre over charcoal. A horse emerges
from the bovine heart.


5   Signature
*Pech-Merle*

He presses his inked hands onto rock
or he blows the deep red ochre through a bone pipe
around his fingers and palm
leaving bare stone in the shape of his hand,
the artist's sign: "I'm here" 17,000 years before,
trembling, I reach mine, almost exactly his size,
as close as I can,
less than a meter beween me
and the dawn of art.

*Elegies*

# Retelling the history

I lie perfectly still
in the humid heat
and let the fan stir up
the air and the stories
Aunt Idy would have told me
if she hadn't died this week.
She was the last among
my grandma's four, the only one
who stepped back into the old
country and brought a husband
home with her.

Now my cousins gather in her room,
sprawled on the floral spread,
the fan turning to each of us,
spinning its blades, bidding
us speak about those days,
like looking at something
familiar through a silver haze,
through layers of veils, and of course,
no one agrees. Whether grandpa
loved my grandma, as she said,
or needed her savings for
the passage here. The fan tumbles
the air, jumbles our words,
the stories twist again
and pass along like tangled jewels,
faded rugs, the love seat
with the ivory silk brocade.

Nearby, hovering, my aunt,
mother, grandma, uncles
vie with each other
for a better view, squabbling
as they always did, nodding,

rooting for the version they prefer.
Who knows what's right? Who cares?
The cousins play cat's cradle
with the string of tales, move
a finger, change designs.
Lovingly, with humor, we repair
the family stories out of myth,
rumor, threadbare anecdotes,
out of the humming air.

# Traub, from my grandma's words

A small village.
A few huts, their roofs
thatched with straw
and when you stoke
the fire, often
the sparks leap
into the straw
and the huts burn.
Traub. Each night
poppies bloom, an
orange light rises
over the village.
Winter. Summer.
The tongues of flames
jab at the icy stars.
Heat. And the heaven
glows like a pomegranate.
Shouts. Shadows,
the dark forms
of families rushing
for the well, pails
passed, a hiss.
The stew expires.
Potatoes scorch
in ash, another hut
opens like a child's mouth
to the Russian sky.

# Henry's Lupine
*for Henry Haskell, Tenant's Harbor, Maine*

Below Henry's house, old radical Henry
who almost died last winter, and just above
the new dock, still blond, unweathered,
the lupine rise, march, bend, inventing
blue again, as if sky shattered, attached
itself to stalks and sticks, standing tall,
spikes of blue beaks, too tall really for flowers,
every blue shade, sky-flakes, sea-drop petals,
stones of lapis, thousands of lupine parade,
lupine fading to pinks, white, violet,
pale blue, mild blue, deep blue, blue purple,
vast fields of blue lupine in June the sick heart
can't resist, lupine ladders tying heaven to earth.
We don't know what made Henry well again,
but there he is proud and strong between his lupine
and the harbor. Straight as any stem.

# There's Millicent in the Small Carved Box
*for Millicent Gordon, 11/10/95*

at the head of her husband's stone
on a fine ridge looking over the Farmington Valley.
The box is cedar, its edges dovetailed, joined
like sisters, elegantly laced.
Inside, her ashes lie still, yet *she* does not.
Leaves glide and lift into November sun,
scarves of blackbirds ride the flyways
dipping and creasing over the bleached fields,
and just below, the river flows darkly.
Hannah coos and reaches toward the box
of ash, the wood's grain tempting as a feather.
Sisters, their past and current husbands, cousins
Jen, Ali, Andrew, Jess, Lewis, Nina, Sam
move among the grave stones
tracing names and dates, releasing stories
from granite like water, like manna.
Arms extend, fingers press.
A wrinkled oak leaf settles in the black river
resting now...riding the foam downstream.

## ROUTINE FOR LEON COLLINS
*Renowned tap dancer and founder of our local studio*

Leon, Leon, you toodling down
the piano keys, whapping at
your axe strings, you strutting
out on the boards
all simple, dressed
sort of ordinary
and out of those ankles
out of those heels and toes
some clickety clicking
like no one ever heard
like some train inexorably
speeding down the track
like some bird trapped
in your patent shoes
and you don't even seem
to move when you make
your heart-breaking blues,
all slow, each foot phrase
hanging in air, clear
as a winter constellation
and as high, hey you
flying out there, jazz
like Ella scatting,
only metal on wood,
your tendons like some
hummingbird, whew Leon
too many taps to count,
a silence like white
light startles, everyone's
clapping and you're down

on your knees, we're
screaming, you're up hey Leon, you've got all the peoples'
hearts, all the peoples' heat
throbbing in your feet,
we're calling for you now,
Leon, encore! What you brought us
that sweet street music, that funk
will stick smack center in our gut,
even now, you're tugging us out
of our chairs, ankles wagging
warming up, a flutter
about the toes, uhuh Leon,
we're going to carry on
and you'll be nodding and shiny
laughing down on us, oh yeah!

# ELEGY FOR ETHERIDGE
*for Etheridge Knight, 3/16/98*

Lots of hats, lots of feathers, net and felt, lots of suits, striped and shiny, shoes that reflect, lots of respect and lots of hips and breasts, babies in blue lace, folks packed into pews so close they couldn't stand up unless they all rose at once, and lots of words, soft at first, then spiraling up electric with the Lord and the joyful passing into His hands, lots of singing Precious Lord with the voice running all around one note and scraping the top ones with a cracking and weeping, lots of yeahing and moaning and amens, uhuh! lots of pastors, sisters and brothers both, and elders, and visiting ministers and Reverend Boniface, the college President saying "Etheridge, our own shine, our own trickster, Etheridge—in the words of the deceased himself—done boogied!" and Etheridge, prettied up under the desk light of the preacher in front of us all, elegant as a Vogue model in a pressed Tweed suit, his Palestinian scarf, his African hat and Navajo beads, is black and smooth as ebony without his scars and stitches, as if he were a black linen letter being drawn out of a white satin envelope and the mourners led from the pews, row by row to read him, guided toward grief with a firm hand at the elbow, even the crumpled mama persuaded to rise up, rise up one more time out of the first seat, to hobble up for a last good-bye and the church nurses crisp and attentive flanking the coffin, poised with tissues and fans, the sobs and wails, the bowing and shaking and the choir singing, "I am free, free," while the reverent file back to their pews, the African hat, the scarf removed and the lid of the coffin closed over the body, the rigid body of the poet, but not over his hot, veiny, fleshy, harsh, free, singing, singular, breathing words.

## At the Cemetery
*for Ida Shoag*

The country road I never knew grows too familiar now.
I recognize the turn-off by the red brick farm,
bear left at the fork, past the valley of cows, right
at the pear grove to the top of the rolling hills.
Walk through a sunny haze, open the iron gate,
pass among granite stones. Stop. While the family dwindles,
the family plot takes shape. My cousins, once boys,
bear the casket to the grave, Aunt Idy, who started stories
in the middle of a phrase, my aunt who meant to sing,
to fly, is tucked between her husband and my mom.

We chant the prayers. Her children sprinkle earth
upon the wood. The wind blows, the pastures
stretch out green. No one wants to leave it seems.
We drift among the headstones piling pebbles
on the mounds, muttering names, fingering the engraved
letters as if they were the faces we loved, my mother Roz,
my uncles Ted and Ben, grandma Mariasha, grandpa Frank.

No one's left in town, the old houses sold,
the cousins gone to live their lives apart, out
from under the power of the family hand.
This now, is home. These plots. A sweet
warmth rises from the land.

## BIRTHDAY WISH
*for Roz and Mayer*

Look at all this light, this gold, rising out of maple
and elm, the red edges of Kousa dogwood, hedges
burning crimson, light running along the dark

bark of cherry. Trace how the palms
of downed leaves reveal our brittle life-lines,
sapped veins, codes for decomposing.

My birthday has just passed and it's wearing how
my parents never call to wish me well;
both dead, their absence sharpens.

This November day, still mild, cannot rouse them
from the damp soil, their polished headstones,
our token pebbles and blue glass gestures.

Shouldn't their dark wings be spread catching
November wind? Autumn day of birth,
release my parents from their night,

speak them into leaves gnawed with stories,
tumbling over each other, gliding, skittering,
into an afterlife filled with light like this.

# Writing My Will

## Early spring walk at the reservoir

Colder than I expected. Wind
        off the water. Spring's too early,
                chartreuse willow fronds drag

on old leaves, bright forsythia beaks
        sip sun and grudgingly open, cherry petals
                are wrapped still in tough buds.

                I know that only love matters.

The cardinal, scarlet against
        the drab grass, is nothing
                if there is no one home to tell.

Earth is thawed, exposed. Bluets
        roam and flow beneath the trees
                whose broken limbs lie scattered. I am raw

with what is almost lost. Oncoming
        walkers nod to a face, a habit
                of circling that might, after all

cease. Day and night, though,
        the slow sap rises and the cherries
                have no choice but to thrive.

# Form and content

Let's be honest,
the skin does not do what it once did,
hold in the body firmly as an avocado,
tight and smooth as a mango,
lean and flexible as willow.

Now the hands are a delta of veins,
a  mottled landscape of craters,
the skin is a cross hatch of crinkles,
and there's all together too much
flesh, bellying and billowing. Pinch

this skin and it stays, heaved into
ancient ridges of the Appalachians,
rinse this hair against grays,
even disguised, it leaps away
from the scalp like solar flares,

and when we lie together
eager to warm our extremities,
my arm reaching over your spine, I see
the skin of my shoulder, loose, shirred,
my mother's shoulder, not mine.

I stretch my arm, trying to reshape
myself before you notice, but of course,
you have seen the way my skin puckers and drapes,
aging like our children do, so gradually
we wonder how they slipped into adults,

and you are kind about the new role of skin,
how it has its own life, separate from the spirit;
you hum a line of Schubert, say a verse of Yeats,
phrasing that wraps itself firmly around
our aging and will hold.

# Mammogram

"Routine," I answer,
and I'm led to the dressing room
to remove my clothes from the waist up
and on the small counter is *People Magazine*
which features two girls joined at the chest,
nine now, eating, reading, leaping
about at dancing school. Engrossed
I can barely undress, carry
that issue into the X-ray room,
set it down close to me while they flatten
my breast between Plexiglas plates
and tighten the screws.

Two children smile permanently
toward each other, making a stab
at a normal life. I try to relax my shoulder,
tilt my head, hold my breath, hear
the radiation whine through me, searching
for or planting the seed of death.
The two girls, sprung from their seed
cheerful as a double tomato or two marigolds
from a single stem, sleep, wrapped around
the other like wisteria, tangled
in the same dream for all we know.

"Breathe," says the technician then presses
my other breast into the platypus bill
of the machine; again radiation reaches
through me, invisible, dangerous, recording
the landscape beneath my wrinkling skin.

The sisters share a heart, although
I'm not sure I have that right, I can't quite
picture where the heart would rest, in one
rib cavity, or somewhere between them,
open to the air like the heart

of Frida Kahlo, something that keeps
them from being cut apart.
                              I am grasped
by a machine that knows nothing
of the sucking tonguing mouth of the infant
or the lover's adoring hand,
but I am whole, still, unless they spot,
on the gray plowed field of the film,
a terrible brightness eager to grow.
Then I will long for my double
to come home to my body, to shield me
from this nova's frightening glow.

## ACUPUNCTURE OF THE BROKEN HEART

I am lying on a thin table
with many slim pins slipped
beneath my skin
speaking to pressure points;
I am as motionless
as I have ever been, breathing
so gently the pins at the corners
of my eyes barely fall and rise,
the pin in the center of my forehead
is as still as the north star
and in my belly,
I barely sense a crown of thorns.

Dr. Chang, who stuck me quick
as a seamstress pinning a hem,
is in the next room.
I hear a deep voice
rough, sad really, asking,
can you help me doctor, can you help
a broken heart?
                Yes,
says the old healer, we often do.
Breathe and tell your story
while I take your pulse.

I wonder how he'll place
the pins to mend torn love?
I feel the tingle of a message in my veins,
"be well" racing through
the tangle and synapse of my brain,
"be well" in the peritoneum, in the ovaries,
ducts, and the raw reproductive remains.

Here too is the love place,
where the lover enters and wishes
to be welcome, to unpack the bags,
unrestrained and singing loudly
the pearly song.

And I root for the pins
that might soothe my old egg nest,
my battered abdomen, and pray
for the man abandoned
in the next room. In pain we've left
the West and traveled East
to one who knows how tapping
some distant spring
rejoins the broken body,
repairs the broken wing.

## Lighting tapers in Notre Dame

This is not our church,
still it flies away into the heavens
on its cold gray limestone
stacked up in slim gothic vaults

pressed to behave by bones
of buttresses that curve
around the outer air.
We are drawn down the nave

along stones worn concave as palms
by pilgrims and processions
past carvings and crucifixes.
Legions of god-fearing marched out

from this soaring transept,
beyond the ghastly gargoyles
to slaughter the fathers
of my father's fathers.

High above us, stained glass
chips of sky and blood
fuse eyes and lips, confuse
the issue, and in the far

reaches of the apse
a hundred candles drip and flicker
shaking the solemn darkness
of the church itself.

What are they for? my children ask.
You light one to remember
one you've loved who died;
Up close, the wax is so translucent

you see the very words the earth-bound
relatives have sent, the heat
of a rising choir. We drop
our francs into the tin

and take two slender tapers,
touch their wicks to fire:
one for my mother
one for my mother's mother;

moving our mouths in prayer,
we draw down the spirits
of our women with silver hair
making this bit of the cathedral
ours.

# If I should be dying

for any length of time
yes let people come
I want them
but not to sit quietly
rocking or touching
my wrist, and not to perform.
Let them come with their work,
let them bring many drafts
of poems, unfinished songs,
threads of tunes, seeds
of stories, a leaning
into dance, and sketchbooks,
pens, chalk, let them mumble
and be busy inside their own
minds, and I who loved to work,
to hear the hum and click
of words come down, to let free
the goldfinch from the cage, I
will be still, alert for the signs
of the muse, and when it is time
for friends to go, their sparked auras
will engulf me and when it is my time
let small slivers of my ore shine
from the cortex of their art.

# Writing my will

About the matter of my body once I've died—
The spirit's always been of most concern.
I just don't know my children, you decide.

Maybe I'll rest on the rural hill beside
my mother, the warm earth, her freckled arms
about the matter of my body. Once I've died

I won't much care. After you've mourned and cried,
sing the songs I wrote and say the poems
I used to know. My children, you decide

which of the many places that I've loved
my ashes might be scattered if I burn.
It's just a matter of the body. Once I've died

if the season's right, I'll probably reside
at Kezar Lake or ledgy Annisquam;
I just don't know, my children. You decide

what will ease your pain. I'm satisfied
to help the lettuce and the raspberries return
over the matter of my body. Once I've died
I just won't know, my children. You decide.

# Bell buoy

Tide withdraws, the rocks emerge bearded and dark beneath
    bright granite,

Tide returns and the beach pulls the blanket of sea up to
    its chin and rests for a moment, private, mysterious,

The wind shifts sometime during the night, the haze blows
    out like milkweed, the bay turns from white gauze
    to purple saris. The only constant:

the bell buoy clanging in the distance, mindlessly
    like a child humming, or with an urgent report,

it clangs toward the beach and the landing, the ledges
    and the grassy knoll where we perch over Ipswich Bay,

it clangs through our speaking and between the words on the
    pages we read; when the wind dies, we find we must bend
    toward it, catch it like the bright flash of cardinal wings,

it clangs through coffee and hanging the wash, through
    lobster boats thrumming and cranking up pots, it clangs
    through waking in dew and through the starred night,

through damp unidentifiable dreams where it is a train
    waiting, or a death, a fish breaking the surface;
    the bell buoy rises and falls on surges of the sea,

it steadies the coast and the constellations,
    tethers the mockingbird and sparrow, the dragonfly
    and linden seeds to the layer where we abide.

Clang, then, with joy and caution, with welcome and warring,
    ride this lifetime insistently, do not be silent! Know
        the message you came to sing, and sing it!

# October Song

Wild asters and the birds whir over
    in flocks,  Queen Anne's Lace curls up
        by the docks, the tide runs out,
    runs out like it hurts, our step
is so light on this earth.

I love these times alone, thinking
    about how my children have grown,
        and how I come into this age
    illuminated, softened
as the marsh's edge.

And the tide runs out, as forceful
    as birth, as if nothing else mattered
        but rushing away and rushing back in
    twice a day. Our step
is so light on this earth.

We're given October like a gift, the leaves
    on the warp, the light on the weft,
        and the gold drips through
    like cider from the press; we know,
we know that our lives are blessed.

But the tide runs out, runs out like it hurts,
    what were fields of water only hours ago
        are meadows now when the tide
    is low; our step is so light
on the earth. Wild asters. All

we are sure of is change, that maple
    and sumac will turn into flame, this softness
        will pass and the winter be harsh
    till the green shoots push
up through the marsh. And the tide

rushes in like a thirst and will keep
    its rhythm even after our time,
        the seasons, too, will repeat
    their design. Our step
is so light on this earth.

# Notes

"Bathing" (p. 28) and "Traveling"(p. 32). These stories are based on experiences related by Prilly Sanville about her mother's final months woven together with my own experiences.

"Who calls down…"(p. 68). On the day before the Bar Mitzvah, a guest checked into the local hotel as Rosalyn Levin, my mother's maiden name. My mother had died eight years before.

"Closer"(p. 94). last two lines are from "Magic Words" after Nalungiaq *from Songs and Stories of Netsilik Eskimos,* edited by Edward Field.

"Barely Holding"(p. 118). In addition to Alzheimer's, my father also had symptons of Parkinson's Disease.

"A Moment in Every Class"(p. 151). I have been teaching and writing poetry with children of all ages for thirty years.

# ACKNOWLEDGMENTS

"No Answer," *Dark Horse,* and *Her Face in the Mirror,* Jewish Women on Mothers and Daughters, ed. by Fay Moskowitz, "Excuse," "Numbers," in *Dark Horse.*

"If I Should be Dying," "January Thaw," "Roller Skating on My Daughter's Birthday," "Burial," "Birthday Poem for Cheyenne Rose," "Traveling" and "Bathing" in *Sojourner.*

"First Time" and "Departure" in *The Boston Globe,* City Section (December 26, 1999 and January 9, 2000).

"Planting Holland Bulbs," in *Stone Country.*

"A Small Thing" in *Kalliope, (Winter, 1990)* Vol. XII, No. 1 and in *Editor's Choice III: Fiction, Poetry, & Art from the U.S. Small Press (1984-1990),* ed. Morty Sklar and Mary Biggs, 1991.

"The Lake," "Wild Things," "What Memories Will Rise," "October Song" on cassette tape, *Feel Yourself in Motion,* Troubadour Productions, 1986.

"The Wind" in *Wordworks Winners, A Retrospective, of the Washington Prize,* ed. Alenier, Tham, and Moore, Wordworks, Washington, DC, 1999.

"Touching Down," and "My Mother Comes Back to Life," in *Worcester Review* (Winter 1989).

"Lighting Tapers in Notre Dame," *Kalliope* (Winter 1990).

"Forsythia" in *Reflections,* Brookline, MA

"Long Distance" in *Revisions,* Talking Stone Press, 1998.

"Lost and Found, A Story" in the *Jewish Women's Literary Annual,* Vol. 3, 1998.

"Meeting the Birthmother" and "Letter with No Address" in *A Ghost at Heart's Edge Stories and Poems of Adoption,* eds. Susan Ito and Tina Cervin, North Atlantic Books, 1999.

"Heirloom" in *Poiesis,* Vol. 2, 2000 and "War Stories" in *Poiesis* Vol. 2, 2001.

My deep appreciation to Robert Kroin, Elizabeth McKim, Ann Phillips and Tom Garfield for their careful readings and insights regarding this collection and to Barbara Emmel Wolinsky for her design guidance.

I am grateful to the Bunting Institute at Radcliffe College for the quiet office and professional support during my fellowship year, 1996/97, and for the porch at Towanah surrounded by white pines, goldfinch, hummingbirds and the healing waters of Kezar Lake.

IN HER FOURTH COLLECTION, Steinbergh sorts through her valuables: the stories, relationships, connections to the natural world, images, sounds, and words she inherited, borrowed or wishes to pass along. In her universe, elements recede, disappear and return. Language itself creates and rescues. Form shapes content, the body of thought and feeling. Throughout her lyrical exploration of loss, search, birth, and connection, her vital *will* shines through.

*Photo by Susan Wilson*

JUDITH W. STEINBERGH has worked since 1971 as Poet-in-the Schools throughout Massachusetts. She has taught, lectured and read at numerous Boston area colleges and through Teachers as Scholars. Judith won the 1983 Washington Prize. Her manuscripts have been finalists in the AWP, Brittingham and San Jose competitions. She was a Massachusetts Council on the Arts and Humanities finalist in fiction, and a Bunting Institute Fellow at Radcliffe in 1996/97.